COMPLETE GUIDE TO
RUNNING

COMPLETE GUIDE TO
RUNNING

JIM ALFORD · BOB HOLMES
RON HILL · HARRY WILSON

 Sterling Publishing Co., Inc. New York

*To the runner who always strives for his
  best and tries to achieve more.*

Acknowledgements
The Publisher would like to thank the following for their help in
the preparation of this book: Josephine White, Phil Norgate,
Michael Woods, Martin Coughlan, Rob Green, Kim Robinson,
Alison Sullivan, The Sweat Shop, Ron Hill Sports Ltd, Adidas,
Nike International, Stuart Perry, Howard Payne, Peter Loughran
and Mark Shearman.

First Published in 1985 by
Sterling Publishing Co., Inc.
Two Park Avenue
New York, N.Y. 10016

ISBN 0-8069-7964-X

Printed in Spain

Contents

Introduction

Running breeds a competitive spirit, which manifests itself in everyone from the Olympic competitor to the fun runner. There is always a desire to test oneself against other athletes whether in a race or unofficially in a training run. Even if an athlete does not have the total competitive winning drive there is always the challenge to run faster or further. Ultimately all serious runners will aim to improve their speed and competitiveness.

Running is a wide-ranging sport, and in this book we are considering the events from 800m upwards. While the disciplines of track running, cross country, road running, the marathon and ultra distance are different, the underlying principles of physiology and training are the same.

Our team of experts draw from a wealth of experience: Harry Wilson and Jim Alford with years of coaching track athletes at international level, Ron Hill with his personal experiences as a world class marathoner and Bob Holmes as a leading light in the ultra-distance revival.

While each section is aimed at runners in each branch of the sport, you the runner can find ways to improve your performance and broaden your experience. The physiology and training techniques of track running as explained by Harry Wilson apply both to road running and marathons; the aerobic and anaerobic principles also apply to both, and the speed training of the track athlete will benefit the road runner.

Today the leading road and marathon runners are drawn from athletes who have made careers on the track and who have specialized in road running. There are now signs that some road runners are taking to the track. Our aim is not only to help you to improve at your event but to give you an insight into those in which you could compete.

Middle-distance track running

Locomotion, for all living creatures, is a natural activity. The bodily movements are innate, instinctive, and the child is already acquiring them while still in the mother's womb. The newly born baby already possesses the neural pathways which govern the intricate co-ordinating movements of arms and legs, but still needs many months to gain the strength and balance needed for running. It is perfectly natural to run and it is perfectly natural for some people to run fast; they are endowed, by nature, with the favourable type of muscle fibre, bodily proportion, joint leverage, power to weight ratio and cardio-vascular potential—but, of course, it is not just natural to perform as well as the world champions do. Great runners are all endowed, in their different ways, by nature, but it still takes many months and years of hard, dedicated and purposeful training for them to reach their true potential.

Technique, in the middle- and long-distance events, is concerned mainly with strategy and tactics. That is not to say that the distance runner is unaware of the importance of efficient movement; after all, no athletes practise the movements of their events more than distance runners and they are very conscious of the need to conserve energy and to avoid wasteful movements—to get speed with the minimum outlay of energy. But improved performance is mostly a matter of conditioning, of improving physical and mental qualities.

It is customary to divide the track events into 'sprinting', 'middle' and 'long-distance' running, although these divisions are quite arbitrary. For example, just 20 years ago, Bresnahan and Tuttle, widely regarded as the foremost authorities in athletics in the USA, classified the middle-distance races as 440 yd and 880 yd, and the long-distance races as one and two miles. In the first AAA booklet, published in 1951, the author took the view that 'middle-distance running' could embrace all flat track races, from the 800m to the 10,000m, with the 800m and the 1500m as the 'short' middle distances and the 5000m and 10,000m as 'long' middle distances.

The East Germans, according to their text book *Leichtathletik*, edited by Gerhardt Schmolensky, classify the middle distances as the 800m and 1500m and the long distances as the 5000m, 10,000m and marathon, although they also quote Satziorski as giving a much more complex definition. Taking the aerobic/anaerobic content of each race as a guide, it would seem logical to consider the 800m as the true middle-distance race, the 1500m as a 'long' middle-distance race, the 5000m as a 'short' long-distance race, the 10,000m as a long-distance race and the marathon as a very long-distance race, and this is roughly what Satziorski has done. Fred Wilt, one of the foremost American track and field authorities, takes a similar view.

Of course, there are many examples of runners who display great ability over a wide range of these distances; this versatility, in fact, is the hallmark of the really great middle-distance runner and it is not just a modern phenomenon. Back in the 1880s Walter George held world records for one mile, three miles and six miles; in the 1920s Paavo Nurmi broke 15 world records, ranging from the 1500m to the 10,000m; in the 1930s and 1940s Sidney Wooderson held world records for 880 yd, 800m and the one mile, took the English National Cross-Country title and, as a finishing flourish to his career, ran away with the European 5000m title. Between 1955 and 1956, the great Hungarian runner, Sandor Iharos, broke seven world records, ranging from 1500m to 10,000m.

Top right Paavo Nurmi competing in October 1923.
Bottom right Sidney Wooderson qualifying for the finals of the AAA mile championship in the 1930s.

Top Sandor Iharos of Hungary wins the 3000m at the British Games at the White City in a new all-comers record of 8 min. 26 sec. **Left** Sidney Wooderson breasts the tape in an international half-mile race at the White City Stadium on 1 August 1938. **Above** Three weeks later, he is held aloft after breaking the half-mile record at a club meeting at Motspur Park, Surrey.

Undoubtedly the pre-eminence of these giants of the past owed something to the fact that very few other runners of their era were willing to train as hard and as often as they did. Nowadays, thousands of runners put in as much training as the world champions, and often on similar lines; competition has now become so much fiercer and more widespread that the most today's champions can hope for is to double up, as Juantorena did in the 400m and 800m, Coe, Ovett and Cram in the 800m and 1500m, and Viren and Yifter in the 5000m and 10,000m.

The basic principles for all these events are much the same; the obvious differences in the running action employed, apart from those due to individual variations in physique, are merely an indication of the proportional emphasis on speed or on endurance. However, the elements of speed and endurance, and the nervous and physical stress entailed, vary so much that the tactics employed for each race deserve separate consideration.

Principles of training

The middle-distance events are often described as non-technical, mainly because the runner's technique is a relatively simple one when compared with the techniques used by hammer throwers, pole-vaulters, triple jumpers and other field-event athletes. However, there is nothing simple about the middle-distance events as soon as we begin to study the physiology and psychology that play such a large part in the athlete's attempt to improve. Improved track surfaces, lighter and better shoes, and more beneficial diets are just some of the factors that have played a part in the incredibly high standards that are now reached by world class runners; but the greatest advances have been achieved by the use of improved training methods and the stimulation of mental attitudes.

Athletes now accept, and adapt to, training loads which at one time would have been thought impossible, and at the same time attempt to record racing times beyond the comprehension of track experts of just 25–30 years ago.

The world record times of 1 min. 41.73 sec. for 800m by Sebastian Coe, 3 min. 30.77 sec. for 1500m by Steve Ovett and 13 min. 00.42 sec. for 5000m by David Moorcroft are staggering performances, but really not so surprising if one were to compare the training of these fine British runners with the training of the world record holders of 1953.

Left *Steve Scott (938) is tracked by Sebastian Coe in the 1984 Olympic 1500m final, as José Abascal (219) runs wide.*

Opposite Alberto Juantorena, 400m and 800m Olympic champion in 1976. **Above left** Dave Moorcroft, the world record holder at 5000m. **Above right** New Zealand's Dick Quax leads Lasse Viren in a 5000m heat at the Montreal Olympics.

But these three runners are typical examples of what we will find if we start to examine the training of successful runners; they use the same training ingredients but there is a wide variation in the emphasis placed on each one.

The basic principle behind physical training is that the body will not just adapt to stresses placed upon it, but will over-compensate so that greater stresses can be withstood. That is why any training programme must be progressive in its intensity, and time must be allowed for the body to adapt to training loads. While some young runners may get good results quite quickly once they start training, it will be several years before the real benefits of training are realized.

The physiology of training

There are three energy systems involved in middle-distance running, and the majority of a runner's time will be spent in trying to improve the efficiency of these three systems. Two of the energy systems are anaerobic processes (without oxygen), and the other is an aerobic process (with oxygen). A splitting of chemical molecules provides the energy for the first $5\frac{1}{2}$ seconds of running and, as no lactic acid is formed in this process, we can describe it as an alactacid anaerobic process. The improvement of this process is valuable to a degree in all running, but obviously has great significance to a 100m runner and very little significance to a 10,000m runner.

The lactacid anaerobic process
For intense running of longer than $5\frac{1}{2}$ seconds' duration, the demand for energy is met by the utilization of the glycogen which is stored within the muscles. However, because of the lack of oxygen, flat-out running would have to end after approximately 40 seconds owing to the depletion of the glycogen supply and the accumulation of lactic acid from the breakdown of the glycogen.

The aerobic process
For longer periods of less intensive running, the intake of oxygen forms part of the energy process and, providing the work is not too intense, the oxygen uptake is sufficient and there are good stores of glycogen, then the work can be maintained for

extremely long periods of time. However, if the work is too intense and the oxygen uptake is insufficient, then there will be a gradual build-up of oxygen debt until the energy process then becomes a lactacid anaerobic one. We can measure the oxygen cost of running at a certain pace and we can also measure the oxygen uptake of an athlete when running at that pace, so we can calculate the oxygen debt (if any) that is building up during the duration of a run. Each person can only tolerate a certain amount of oxygen debt, but this tolerance level is much higher in a trained runner (about 17 litres) than in an untrained runner (about 10 litres).

As an example, and to quote Dr Ray Watson, Head of Human Sciences at Brighton Polytechnic, 'A mile run at a pace of 60 seconds per lap will cost about 8.7 litres per minute or 34.8 litres of total oxygen cost for the four minute run. If an athlete attempting the race has a maximum oxygen uptake of four litres per minute, as well as an oxygen debt capacity of 17 litres,

the total oxygen available would be $(4 \times 4) + 17 = 33$ litres and the four-minute mile would be beyond the runner's physiological capacity.'

So it is in a runner's interest to stay out of oxygen debt for as long as possible by using the aerobic process, and the ability to do this will depend largely on his oxygen uptake. Other factors, such as using an efficient technique and not running in an energy-wasting way, also assist but, inevitably, if the pace of the runner is fast and prolonged then the lactacid anaerobic process will be utilized.

So runners today must be conditioned to withstand as large an oxygen debt as possible. With training we endeavour to increase an athlete's oxygen uptake and tolerance to lactic acid, but we must always remember that the amount of improvement that can be made will depend on certain natural attributes possessed by each individual athlete. In particular we are concerned with the quality of a person's skeletal muscle fibres.

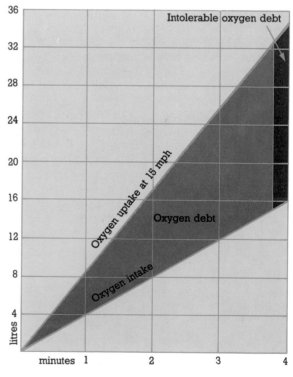

Above *Oxygen debt. The shaded portion of the diagram shows oxygen debt occurs when the uptake of oxygen (shown here at four-minute mile pace) is greater than the oxygen intake (this athlete has an intake of 4 litres/minute). An athlete can tolerate some oxygen debt; for a trained athlete who can tolerate a debt of 17 litres, he would not be able to go any further at that pace than the portion shaded orange.* Left *Australia's Herb Elliott looks in distress as he wins the final of the Olympic 1500 m at Rome in 1960.*

Muscle fibres

The human muscular system consists of a mixture of slow-twitch red fibres and fast-twitch white fibres. A heavy predominance of slow-twitch fibres means a runner is more suited to endurance events, whereas an athlete who has a greater predominance of fast-twitch fibres will do better in the explosive sprinting events. If we carried out muscle biopsies on marathon runners we would expect to see as much as 95% of red fibres, but similar biopsies on sprinters could quite likely reveal a similar percentage of white fibres. It does not need much imagination to work out that such gifted runners as Steve Ovett and Sebastian Coe who possess both great speed and stamina would almost certainly have a near 50:50 ratio of the two types of fibre. If a runner is naturally endowed with a high proportion of slow-twitch fibres then it follows that intelligent training can bring about a big increase in oxygen uptake, but no amount of endurance training can bring about a significant increase in oxygen uptake if an athlete has only a very small amount of slow-twitch fibres. So while the type of training must be related to the aerobic and anaerobic requirements of an event, it must also be related to each athlete's physiological assets. It is vital for each athlete to analyse the needs of a particular event and also to analyse what he himself has to offer. It is not necessary to carry out a muscle biopsy in order to determine an athlete's muscular make-up.

If a person can perform an endurance activity such as running or cycling for long periods of time without much fatigue, then it is more than likely that he possesses a good supply of slow-twitch fibres. If this person performs very badly in explosive activities then obviously he should be directed towards the longer endurance events, 10,000m to marathon. However, if a person tires very quickly after attempting such activities but is at ease with explosive forms of exercise such as sprinting, jumping or weight lifting, then a high proportion of fast-twitch fibres is indicated, and the athlete is unlikely to do well at endurance running.

When you find a person who does very well at both endurance and explosive activities then you have an ideal middle-distance runner (800–5000m) and one who will almost certainly have a fairly even ratio of the two types of fibre. When we refer to a runner as being 'a natural' we mean one who not only possesses the right ratio of muscle fibres to suit a particular event, but also one who has been endowed with large quantities of these fibres. This explains why a natural runner such as Steve Ovett, who is naturally suited to

Right *Steve Ovett, 800m gold medallist and 1500m bronze medallist at the Moscow Olympics and world record holder at 1500m and two miles, was unable to compete effectively in the 1984 Olympic finals because of health problems.*

the middle-distance events, can still do better than most runners at the long-distance events. Although many of these long-distance runners may possess a more correct ratio of muscular fibres for the longer runs, Ovett's sheer quantity of slow-twitch fibres is sufficient for him to produce better results. As an example, one million fibres divided 50:50 gives half a million slow-twitch fibres; 600,000 fibres divided into one third fast twitch and two thirds slow twitch still gives only 400,000 slow fibres.

So it is vital that an athlete takes the right attributes to an event or he is in for many frustrations and heartaches. The author trained to be a 400m runner for several years with little success; then one year, after switching to endurance running, he gained an International Cross Country vest. He had not carefully analysed the needs of the event and what he had to offer.

The physique of the middle-distance runner

Of course, the muscle fibre ratio is not the only asset needed by the successful middle-distance runner. Other physical factors are
(a) A powerful healthy heart that will carry out its work of a pump to carry oxygen-loaded blood to the muscles, then take blood loaded with waste products away from the muscle to the oxygen-restoring lungs.
(b) Large lungs that will inhale large quantities of oxygen-loaded air and extract the oxygen from the air. The action of the lungs is dependent on the efficiency of the inter-costal muscles which will allow a big chest expansion which, in turn, will allow the lungs to expand as they take in the large quantities of air.
(c) A well proportioned frame. Ideally we are looking for long legs that spring from a short, light but powerful torso and to which are attached big powerful feet. Shoulders should be wide, hips narrow, arms light but strong and not too long. However, not many runners possess this ideal frame, but they have still done well because they have been well endowed physiologically.

Training to improve on natural physique

An athlete cannot choose the heart, lungs and frame that he is born with, but he can endeavour to make the best use of these natural assets. The heart is a muscle and, like any other muscle, responds and adapts to training, so it is not surprising that a middle-distance runner's heart will become larger than an average person's heart. This is an effect to be welcomed, not feared as in early medical days.

The reader will note that the phrase 'other *physical* factors' was used earlier on in this chapter, as psycho-logical factors also play a major part in the development of a good middle-distance runner. Many young athletes who seem to have great natural physical talent fail to capitalize on this talent because of a lack of determination and discipline, while many runners who seem less gifted physically have done extremely well because they are mentally tough. When we have an athlete who possesses great natural physical talent, and allies discipline and determination with this talent, then we witness the development of a great runner.

So we can list the various advances that a runner will attempt to make as a result of training, then consider each point in greater depth later on.

Below John Walker of New Zealand, 1500m gold medallist at the Montreal Olympics and for a decade a world-class middle-distance athlete, leads John Robson at Brisbane in 1982.
Opposite Sebastian Coe, world record holder at 800m and the mile.

(a) An improvement in basic speed, i.e. his ability to sprint fast. This asset is greatly influenced by leg strength and mobility in the lower limbs.

(b) The development of good running techniques —when cruising during the major part and when accelerating during the course of a race or sprinting at the finish. The sprinting technique is concerned only with efficiency, but the cruising technique must be economical as well as efficient.

(c) An improvement in oxygen uptake. This factor will probably account for the greatest improvement in an athlete's performance.

(d) An improvement in oxygen debt tolerance. This is the other major improvement that comes about as a result of training and it varies in importance according to the distance raced and the speeds achieved. Obviously the shorter the distance raced the faster the speed involved and the inevitability of oxygen debt occurring. In a very fast 800m we can imagine a runner starting to go into oxygen debt before 50% of the race has been completed, so he has quite a large proportion of the race to cover with the lactacid anaerobic process. In contrast, the 10,000m runner may only use this process for a very small portion of the race—usually towards the finish as the pace increases considerably. Although the 10,000m runner may quite often cover most of his run aerobically, we can imagine that a very fast start or fast surges during the course of a race may cause a lactic acid build-up which has to be cleared quickly as the race proceeds. Some years ago calculations were made taking into account the oxygen requirements of an event, the likely oxygen uptake by a trained athlete during this event, and the subsequent oxygen debt incurred. From these calculations we can draw up a table showing the relationships between the various types of energy processes and this table is quoted below.

However, it must not be assumed that the percentages shown are the ratios that should be followed when deciding the amount of training time to devote to different energy processes; although the figures in the oxygen requirements column may be fairly con-stant, the figures in the next two columns will vary from athlete to athlete according to each person's own individual oxygen uptake and oxygen debt tolerance. The greater the oxygen uptake the less the oxygen debt with a subsequent reduction of the anaerobic factor. This point has become more accepted in recent times and has resulted in 800m and 1500m runners including much more aerobic work in their training. In the past people looked at the above percentages and said 'well if the anaerobic content of a race appears to be 66% then roughly two thirds of an athlete's training should be concerned with this energy process'. Now, by using large amounts of aerobic work, we can delay the onset of the anaerobic process. You may use the analogy of a car driver setting out to make a journey knowing that he has insufficient fuel to last the distance. One can merely tell him what to do when he eventually runs out of fuel. The author would prefer to advise him first of all how to drive economically so as to make the fuel last out for as long as possible, then advise on the steps to take when the fuel eventually runs out. So a runner should try to delay the onset of the anaerobic process rather than just try to build up his tolerance to lactic acid.

Running technique

The technique used by a runner for the major part of a race must be mechanically sound but it must also be economical, so it is important to consider the various factors that contribute to an efficient 'cruising-style'. The photo sequences on pages 72–77 show very efficient actions and additional information accompanies the pictures. However, the following points are worth stressing.

Leg action

1. The knees should point straight ahead and any turning in or out of the knees will result in the feet being planted in a similar out-of-alignment manner. This means that instead of all drive being in a forward direction a certain amount of drive is being directed

Table showing the inter-relationship between aerobic and anaerobic work for running events						
Event (metres)	Characteristic	Total oxygen requirement (litres)	Actual oxygen intake (litres)	Oxygen debt (litres)	Type of work	Approx. % anaerobic/ aerobic
800	Anaerobic, aerobic endurance, speed	26	9.0	17	Anaerobic, aerobic	67% 33%
1500	Anaerobic, aerobic endurance, speed	36	19	17	Anaerobic, aerobic	45% 55%
5000	Aerobic endurance	80	63	17	Anaerobic, aerobic	20% 80%
10,000	Aerobic endurance	150	130+	17	Anaerobic, aerobic	10% 90%

to the left and right. Lack of strength in the thighs is usually the cause of turned-out knees, and hill-running is recommended to remedy this weakness in addition to some specific strengthening exercises. Two different types of hill-training are suggested:

(a) Running fairly fast up a gently sloping hill (10–15 degrees) for about 400–500m. The runner should attempt to maintain a normal-length stride and as the legs tire towards the end of each run he must resist the temptation to shorten the stride. Knees should point ahead and the body should not be allowed to adopt an exaggerated forward lean. It is vital to remember that the object of these hill runs is to gain leg strength and not to get fast times. Six to eight repetitions are suggested with an easy jog back down between repetitions.

Hill running is recommended to build up leg muscles and overall strength.

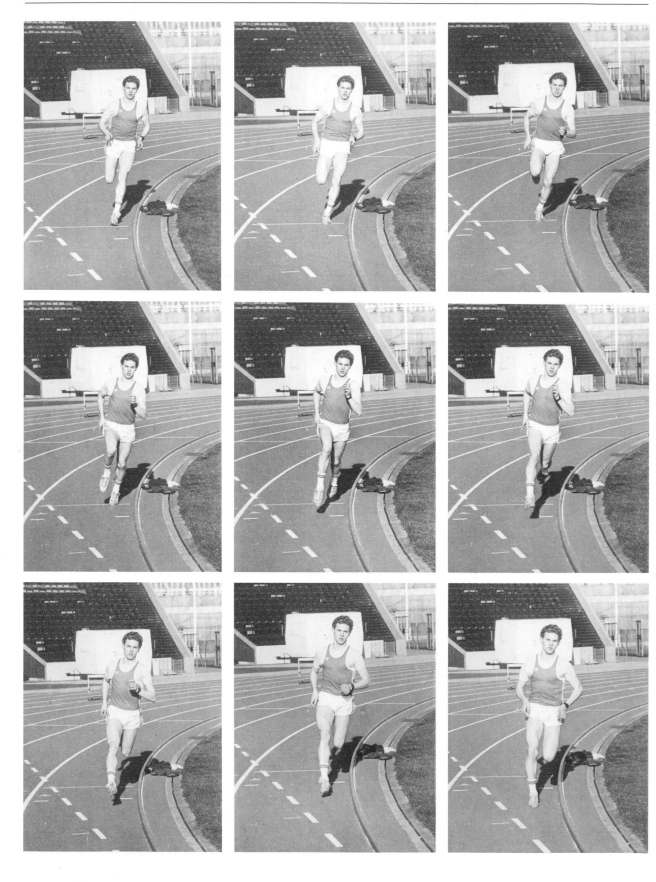

(b) Sprinting up a steeper hill (about 15–20 degrees) about 100–150m in length. The runner will need to have an exaggerated thigh lift in order to sprint, so a full and powerful arm action will be needed to balance this violent leg action. Emphasis is placed on maintaining a high and straight knee lift throughout each run. Ten to twelve repetitions are suggested with a slow walk back between each sprint.

2. While stride length is mainly determined by the work done by the calves and thighs, great assistance can be given by correct use of the feet. For most of the time a middle-distance runner lands lightly on his heels then rolls forward to complete the leg drive from the back of the foot. However, some 'flat-footed' runners land heavily on the heel and fail to roll forward and drive off from the front of the foot;

Opposite *Phil Norgate demonstrates an economical and efficient middle-distance running action. The arms are carried correctly and swing lightly across the torso. The knees point to the front and the runner is looking at the track several yards in front. Note the way the outside of the foot touches the ground first.*

Below *Fast running up stadium steps is a good alternative to hill running. Jo White here shows clearly the exaggerated technique that is required.* **Overleaf** *It is vital that middle-distance runners practise sprinting, and Phil Norgate shows the full range of movement that we expect to see in a sprinter.*

therefore the foot is not used as another lever to assist the leg drive and the athlete loses a little in stride length. This fault can usually be attributed to weak or stiff calf muscles or immobile ankle joints. The hill runs mentioned previously will help to strengthen the calves, but a runner who suffers from this fault will also need to include exercises to gain more range in the calves and ankles. Some useful exercises are shown in the section on mobility, and running over soft uneven surfaces will also develop strength and mobility in the ankles.

Failure to use the feet correctly or running with the knees turned out may only affect each stride by a small amount, but when this is multiplied several hundred times during a race then the amount lost can be significant. This is why it is important to eradicate faults right at the beginning of a runner's career as it becomes almost impossible to alter a technique that has been formed during the thousands of strides that an athlete uses in his training.

A good technique is particularly needed in a sprint finish or if a fast burst is used during the course of a race, and it is on these occasions that a lack of leg strength or mobility becomes most apparent. The thighs must be raised high in order to allow the full extension of the driving legs and the drive must be extended right through the feet to the toes. In addition to practising the specific exercises for gaining strength and mobility, the middle-distance runner must also practise his sprinting technique, and some sprinting drills are described in the section on improving speed.

Arm action

In the middle-distance events a good running technique means an economical use of energy, but energy is often wasted by unnecessary arm movements. If we bear in mind the point that a runner's arm action acts as the balance to his leg action, then it is fairly easy to imagine the sort of movements that are needed. When the leg action is vicious and powerful, as in the 100m sprint, then a powerful, violent arm action is required, but a relaxed, swinging arm action is needed to counterbalance the easy striding action used in the middle-distance events.

For any movement of the legs there is an equal and opposite reaction by the upper part of the body, and the runner must ensure that his arm action gives an economical reaction. If the arms are not used properly then the shoulders will provide the reaction, and shoulder movements are both wasteful and slow (the shoulders and upper part of the body will twist, and it should be noted that much more energy is needed to move these large masses than is needed to swing the lighter arms).

Arms should be flexed at roughly 90° and should swing easily backwards and forwards, slightly across the front of the body. Easy paddling movements of the forearms will have no ill effects, but the elbows should be kept low and close to the body. If the elbows come too far away from the sides, the body and shoulders will develop a wasteful, rolling action.

For the major part of a middle-distance race the arms should be kept low, but a much more powerful action is advocated during the finishing burst. The arms should be raised, flexed more and worked much more violently in an attempt to make the legs react in a similar way. At this stage of a race, speed and not economy is the decisive factor, and it is particularly important to be able to make a quick change into this sprinting action.

The middle-distance man is usually well enough developed to use his arms correctly for the main part of a race, but many runners are not strong enough to be able to adopt the powerful finishing action that has been suggested. It is no good shouting to a runner 'drive your arms' if there are no muscles present to do the driving. If a runner is weak, then specific strength training is the obvious way for him to develop the necessary body strength that will enable him to use his arms properly during all stages of a race, and the exercises suggested are given in the accompanying strength circuit.

Mobility

***Below and overleaf** Jo White demonstrates six exercises that should be carried out daily, each position being held for 15–20 sec. and repeated 3–4 times. Jo shows excellent mobility in maintaining each exercise at the full range of movement.*

Opposite and above A strength/endurance circuit. The three exercises illustrated are carried out in the following sequence: press-ups, sit-ups, and squat thrusts. It is suggested that athletes start by doing each exercise for 20 sec., with 20 sec. rest between each. When progress has been made to 60 sec. of each exercise with 60 sec. rest in between, the athlete can build up to two or three sets of the exercises allowing 2 min. recovery between sets. Press-ups: make sure the body is lowered to the horizontal position, but not allowed to sag. Sit-ups: the trunk is raised then pressed down until the forehead touches the knees. Squat thrusts: the knee should come forward to level with the arms, then should be fully extended to the rear (repeat with each leg).

Improving speed

As each year goes by and the times achieved in the different events become faster, then the ability to sprint becomes more and more important. Obviously basic speed is more important to the 800m runner than to the 10,000m runner but, in all the middle-distance races, a runner may need to call on sheer speed during three sections of a race: to get a good position at the start; to surge or counteract surges during the course of a race; and during a sprint finish. A runner who has little speed is physically limited in the tactics he can employ and he is usually only too psychologically aware of his shortcomings. The need for speed can be seen in different ways at world class level by considering that quite often the first lap of an 800m race will be run in approximately 49 seconds and that, on occasions, the last lap of a 10,000m race can be run in close to 52 seconds.

The most important requirement for a sprinter is to be born with a high proportion of fast-twitch muscle fibres and, although the middle-distance runner may not be naturally blessed with this asset, it is vital for him to improve the quality of the fast fibres that he does possess. The 800m runner needs to emphasize the speed factor more than the 10,000m runner, and he will be one who possesses the greater capabilities for improvement. So the amount of time spent on improving speed is related to the needs of the event and the athlete's potential for improvement. It is a good idea for all runners to include 'speed drills' at the appropriate time of the year and a suggested session would be:

3 × 60m relaxed stride emphasizing good technique
3 × 60m emphasizing high knee lift
3 × 60m emphasizing high heel 'flick-ups'
3 × 60m emphasizing very fast and short strides
3 × 60m starting at an easy pace then gradually accelerating to top speed
3 × 60m flat out from standing start
6 × 60m bounding.

Opposite above High knee lift—a good exercise for leg strength. The runner covers 50–60m moving forward slowly with an exaggerated leg lift. Note the powerful development of the lifting leg and the full extension of the driving foot.
Opposite below Another leg strengthener in which the runner covers 40–50m bounding from alternate legs. The thigh of the lifting leg is held horizontally for as long as possible and the resulting flat-footed landing places a large load on the legs.
Above Flick-ups. The thighs remain almost vertical while the athlete flicks up his heels high and fast.

The photo sequences demonstrate three of these drills clearly. Speed sessions that are specific to different distances are included in the sections on individual events.

Improving oxygen uptake

Oxygen uptake is best improved by aerobic running and this form of training should be carried out at different intensities, and over different distances. Whenever exercise is carried out, the heart beats faster in order to increase the speed of the circulating blood, and measurement of the heart-beat rate will give a good guide to the intensity of the work done. The object of this form of training is to raise the level of the heart rate and to maintain it at a fairly even level throughout the session. The pace of these steady-state runs will depend on an athlete's fitness and on the distance being run, but there is a minimum pace that has to be achieved if the training is to have any effect. This training threshold can be determined by the following method:
(a) record the heart-rate at rest in beats per minute
(b) count the heart-rate in beats per minute immediately after an all-out effort over 300 or 800 metres
(c) the difference between (a) and (b) gives the athlete's pulse range; add two thirds of this figure to the resting figure counted in (a) and this is the heart rate that needs to be reached in order to achieve any training effect.

Running at a rate much less than 10 beats per minute below this training threshold has very little effect. As an example, a runner who has a resting rate of 60 beats per minute and a maximum rate of 180 beats per minute should be doing aerobic work at a rate that will produce a pulse rate of at least 140 beats per minute. The runner should train over a range of distances and at different intensities and, as an example, the runner mentioned in the preceding paragraph would probably be doing aerobic runs such as:
(a) 3 – 5 mile runs at a pace that will produce a pulse rate of approximately 165 beats per minute
(b) 6 – 8 mile runs at a pace that will produce a pulse rate of approximately 155 beats per minute
(c) 8 – 12 mile runs at a pace that will produce a pulse rate of approximately 145 beats per minute.

Main picture *It is valuable for a runner to have company during training runs, but training companions should be chosen so that they are of a reasonably similar standard.* **Inset** *In interval sessions, the coach should check pulse rates to ensure the effectiveness of the training.*

Although steady-state running will form the major part of a runner's aerobic work, some variety can be introduced by running some fairly easy-paced repetitions interspersed with very short recovery periods. Two examples could be (a) 800m runners: 12 × 200m at race pace with 30 sec. jog recovery between each; (b) 5000m runners: 6 × 1000m at race pace with 30 sec. jog recovery between each.

With this type of session the pace is not so intensive that it becomes anaerobic, and the recovery is so short that the pulse drops very little below the training threshold. One can imagine a runner who uses the above sessions recording pulse rates of about 160–165 beats per minute after each fast stretch and pulse rates of about 140–145 beats per minute after the recovery period. This steady-state and near-steady-state running has the effect of moving huge quantities of blood around the circulatory system, and research has shown that this form of exercise produces greater capillarization, i.e. opening up more channels for blood to be carried to and from the working muscles.

The lengths and frequency of the training run vary according to the event raced and the point reached in an athlete's training programme, and examples of the way in which these aerobic runs are used are included in the schedules for the different events.

The body will adapt to this form of training and, in order to maintain progress, the runner will need to increase the distance at which he can maintain a certain pace, increase the pace over distances used previously, and increase the frequency of the runs.

At certain times of the year, usually in periods of intense competition, the runner will not try to increase the intensity of his training by any of the above three methods, but will measure his progress by noting how much easier it is to cover distances in the same times as previously. In this way he knows that he is getting fitter but is not trying to push any harder in training, and is saving intense efforts for races.

It is suggested that some of these aerobic runs are timed so that an athlete can measure how progress is being made and so adjust his pace accordingly. However, he should be careful not to treat each run as a time trial, and he should remember the old but true saying 'train to race—not race to train'.

It is valuable for a runner to have company during his runs but he should choose his training companions carefully. It is not of much benefit to him to train with people who are much slower, particularly if he runs at the pace of the slower runner and fails to get his pulse above the required training threshold. On the other hand, if his fellow trainees are of too high a quality he will find the runs too fast and will not be able to maintain a steady-state pulse, and will not achieve the objective of the training. Ideally a runner would like to be accompanied by someone of a slightly lower standard so that he can maintain his training threshold

without too much effort but can step up the pace if he occasionally needs a very high quality run.

Improving oxygen debt tolerance

In order to encourage the body to adapt to a condition of oxygen debt the runner will need to use the anaerobic energy process in some of his sessions, and training at a fast pace is called for in order to ensure that oxygen requirements will exceed oxygen uptake. Obviously a runner will not be able to maintain a fast or very fast pace for any length of time before either easing off or resting, and the whole concept of anaerobic training is based around the idea of periods of fast running interspersed with recovery periods. The pace and distance of the fast efforts can be raised which in turn affects the duration of the recovery periods. However, once a training session of several repeated fast efforts has commenced, the athlete will only partially recover during the rest periods between the fast efforts, and it will be several hours before full recovery is achieved. The faster the pace and the longer the length of a fast stretch then the higher the pulse rate achieved and, consequently, the longer the time needed to allow the athlete to partially recover.

There are several forms of running practised by a runner to accustom himself to performing under conditions of oxygen debt, the most common being interval running, repetition running, Fartlek, and race-practice or time trials.

Interval running

There are now several and varied forms of interval running, but the original one as conceived by the German partnership of coach Gerschler and physiologist Reindell was to carry out a series of runs over a set distance in a fixed time with a set recovery jog between each fast stretch. A typical session for a 1500m runner with a personal best of 3 min. 40 sec. could be 8 × 400m in 57/58 sec. with a recovery jog of 300m covered in 3 min. between each 400m. The training could be made more intensive by increasing the time of the fast runs, increasing the number of the fast runs, increasing the distance covered in the fast runs or reducing the recovery time between the fast runs. Pulse rates were the yardstick used for measuring the intensity of the fast stretches and the efficiency of the recovery, and the German pair would look for a pulse of approximately 180 beats per minute after the fast effort and approximately 120 beats per minute after the recovery jog. Distances of 100m, 200m, 300m and 400m were originally favoured but later the Germans also used 500m and 600m.

The original concept of using one fixed distance throughout the session is still the one most commonly used, although many athletes use several distances in a training session. An example could be 1 × 600m,

3 × 400m, 4 × 400m, 5 × 300m, with appropriate recovery runs between each.

Although interval running was once regarded as primarily to be carried out on a track, there are now many runners who use the same principle carried out over circuits on grass or in the woods. The author prefers to see runners using circuits away from the track for distances above 400m, and another factor can be added to the training by ensuring that hilly circuits are used. As with any form of physical training, to be effective, interval running must be progressive and, once the body has adapted to and mastered a session of a particular intensity, the session should be made a little more severe. However, an athlete must ensure that he can comfortably handle the number and pace of the fast stretches and recover during the slow jogs before he intensifies the session. In general 800m and 1500m runners should progress by increasing the speed of the fast stretches, but 5000m and 10,000m runners should advance by reducing recovery times, or by increasing the quantity or distance of the fast stretches. The coach should only intensify one factor at a time and it is

unreasonable to expect a runner both to improve the speed of the fast stretches and to reduce recovery times. The coach should make clear to the runner what is the object of the session and should see that the athlete tries to meet his objectives. If he is supposed to do 8 × 400m at 60 seconds a lap with a 3 min. jog in between, he has not achieved his objective if he runs 4 × 400m in. 58 sec. with a 3 min. jog, then has to deteriorate to a further 4 × 400m in 64 sec. with a 4 min. jog between.

What distances should be used? How many fast stretches should be attempted? How fast should the hard efforts be? How much recovery should be allowed? These are the questions asked when contemplating using interval running; although sessions should be tailored to the needs of each individual and the relevant stage, the following training loads are suggested as a general guide. One must always bear in mind that each of the four segments that form an interval training session are closely linked, i.e. the distance used and the speed selected are interlinked, as are the number of repetitions attempted and the recovery time allowed between each fast run.

Interval training session on the track with the coach carrying out timing of the runs.

If a relatively short distance is chosen then the pace needed will be well below race pace for distance, but if a longish distance is involved then the pace will only be a little below race pace. If the pace chosen is very fast then a longish recovery time will be needed, but if the pace is slow then a shorter recovery is called for.

Distances to use and number of repetitions

	800m runner	1500m runner	5000m/10,000m runner
200m	6–8	8–12	–
300m	4–6	5–12	15–24
400m	3–5	6–12	16–24
500m	–	4–6	–
600m	–	3–5	8–12
800m	–	–	8–12

It is definitely recommended that pulse rates should be used to determine the speed of the runs and the length of time allowed for recovery, and these should be in the range of 175–185 beats per minute after the fast efforts and 110–120 beats per minute after the recovery period. One or two counts taken during a session can ensure that the training loads are adequate. Aiming for these pulse rates should ensure that the quality of the run is sufficiently high, and it should be remembered that target times for a particular distance should generally be faster than the athlete's race pace for that distance. As an example, an athlete who runs 800m in 1 min. 56 sec. is covering each consecutive 200m in approximately 29 sec. (without any rest between each 200m) so if he uses this 200m unit in interval training then he must run faster than 29 sec. because he has the advantage of a recovery jog between each 200m. As an athlete gets fitter he usually starts to improve the quality of his interval training automatically but, by checking pulse rates, he or his coach can determine when to intensify the session. As an example, an athlete who starts his interval training by running 8 × 200m in 30 sec. with a 200m jog in 2 min. as a recovery, and is recording pulse rates of 180 and 120 beats per minute, will probably find after a few sessions at this training load that he will then be recording pulse rates of 170 and 110 beats per minute. It is time then to increase the pace or to reduce the recovery.

For distances of more than 400m, it is preferable to use a circuit away from the track for interval training. Interval training on circuits away from the track gives variety and hills can be included.

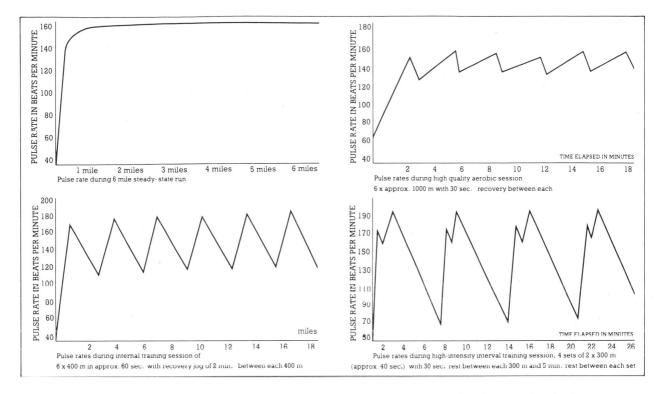

Pulse rate during 6 mile steady-state run

Pulse rates during high quality aerobic session
6 x approx. 1000 m with 30 sec. recovery between each

Pulse rates during internal training session of
6 x 400 m in approx. 60 sec. with recovery jog of 2 min. between each 400 m

Pulse rates during high-intensity interval training session; 4 sets of 2 x 300 m
(approx. 40 sec.) with 30 sec. rest between each 300 m and 5 min. rest between each set

The author has found it valuable with experienced 800m and 1500m runners to include some really intensive interval training in the programme by using short, very fast, repetitions interspersed with very short recoveries. This will mean an athlete can only run a small quantity of these fast runs, so a longer rest is then needed before tackling a further set of repetitions. An example for a first class 1500m runner capable of 3 min. 40 sec. could be five sets of 3 × 200m in 24–25 sec. with a jog of 30 sec. between each 200m followed by a 4–5 min. rest between each set. This type of training could well result in a pulse rate of over 200 beats per minute being achieved at the end of each set, so it is vital that a long rest is allowed between sets in order to give the athlete time to recover.

This particular type of interval training is extremely exhausting both physically and mentally (great concentration is needed to maintain the quality of the fast runs) so such a session is not recommended within five days of a race.

It should be stressed again that interval training must be progressive to be effective and, once an athlete has mastered a particular session and has performed it well two or three times, he must make the session more intensive.

Repetition running

In this type of anaerobic training the athlete uses longer distances than those used in interval training and, as a good pace is used, it follows that a longer

recovery is required and may take the form of complete rest or walking instead of jogging. Because of the length of the repetition and the high quality involved, a formidable amount of lactic acid will accumulate on each run, so it is unreasonable to expect an athlete to attempt many repetitions in each session. Suggested quantities and distances to use for the different events are:

800m, 2–4 × 600m; 2–3 × 1000m

1500m, 3–6 × 800m; 4–6 × 1000m; 2–3 × 1200m

5000m, similar to 1500m plus 2–3 × 2000m

10,000m, 6–8 × 1000m; 4–6 × 1200m; 3–4 × 2000m; 2–3 × 3000m.

Quality is the important factor with repetition running, and the speed used should be as fast or faster than racing pace, depending on the distance used and the number of repetitions performed. If the runner is only attempting two or three repetitions of a particular distance then the pace must be considerably faster than the pace used for that distance in a race. However, if a runner is going to tackle several repetitions then the pace could well be the same as race pace for that distance. Examples could be:
800m runner capable of 2 min.—3 × 600m in 85/86 sec. with 4/5 min. full recovery between.
5000m runner capable of 13 min. 30 sec.—6 × 1000m in 2 min. 42 sec. with 4 min. walk/jog recovery between.

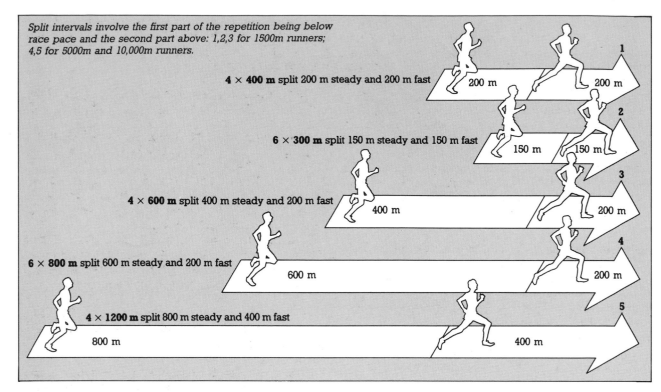

Split intervals involve the first part of the repetition being below race pace and the second part above: 1,2,3 for 1500m runners; 4,5 for 5000m and 10,000m runners.

4 × 400 m split 200 m steady and 200 m fast · 200 m · 200 m · 1

6 × 300 m split 150 m steady and 150 m fast · 150 m · 150 m · 2

4 × 600 m split 400 m steady and 200 m fast · 400 m · 200 m · 3

6 × 800 m split 600 m steady and 200 m fast · 600 m · 200 m · 4

4 × 1200 m split 800 m steady and 400 m fast · 800 m · 400 m · 5

It is suggested that repetition running gradually takes over from interval running as the athlete approaches the peak of his competition season, particularly if the 800m and 1500m events are concerned. Athletes feel that the quality involved and the longer recovery allowed better simulate the sensation they feel in races than in interval running.

Fartlek

This is a Swedish word meaning 'speed-play' and the method of training first became well known in the early 1940s following the world-record-breaking exploits of two of its devotees, the Swedes Arne Anderson and Gundar Haegg. The method had probably been used for many years and by many people prior to this period, but no-one had bothered to give it a name. It is a natural form of training performed best in woods, over the countryside, around golf courses, in parks and other similar areas that provide soft undulating surfaces. The athlete runs for a certain length of time rather than for a set distance and, during the session, he runs fast and slow stretches according to the way he feels and the conditions he encounters. There will be no set distances to run fast; the pace can vary from sprinting to striding at race pace and there will be no predetermined length of time set for the recovery jog he has between the fast surges. He speeds up his run when he feels ready to go again. A typical 50 min. Fartlek session could be: 5 min. jog to park; fast stride over about 800m across a flat field; 2 min. easy jog to recover; three surges of about 1 min. each across an undulating field with 1 min. jog between each; stride at race pace for about 4 min. along a level path; jog for 3 min.; hard run for 600m up a gradual slope; jog for 2 min.; six very fast sprints for about 8–10 sec. on a flat piece of short grass with a jog of about 1 min. between each; 4 min. easy stride across rough fields; jog for 1 min.; four fast repetitions up a steep hill about 50/60m long, jogging back down slowly between each repetition; two easy strides for about 3 min. each across flat country with 1 min. recovery jog after each; a 2 min. run along a patch gradually getting faster and faster; 3 min. recovery jog to finish off.

Although the athlete virtually runs 'as he pleases', he should ensure that there is a good variety of fast running at different speeds and over varied distances and surfaces. As with all other forms of training 'Fartlek' must be progressive and, as the runner gets fitter, so he should increase the number and severity of fast stretches and try to reduce jogging time.

It may be difficult for an inexperienced runner to get the true feel of Fartlek, so he should run a few sessions with a more experienced athlete. But as soon as he appreciates what is required to make the training effective then he should train on his own, becoming his own judge as to the intensity of a session. The runner who uses Fartlek must be honest with himself and must be able to train hard and intelligently without supervision. There is really no such training as 'easy Fartlek' although some sessions are easier than others.

Race practice

This form of training adds another factor to the anaerobic effect, i.e. an attempt to reproduce or nearly produce situations and feelings that happen in a race. The ability to surge when tired; being able to speed up quickly from a slow pace; injecting pace into a race; withstanding a gradual increase of pace; surging, relaxing then surging again—these are all race happenings that can be practised in training. This type of training is best introduced just before the start of the track racing season and can be continued throughout the competition period. The best way to describe the training is to outline some typical race-practice sessions.

Split intervals Here the first part of the repetition is done at a little below race pace, and the final part at above race pace. The athlete can surge in two ways: (a) gradually increasing the pace over the second part of the run, or (b) surging violently at the half-way mark and trying to maintain this pace until the end of the repetition.

Some suggested sessions for runners who can run about 2 min. for the 800m or 4 min. 10 sec. for the 1500m are:

4 × 400m, split first 200m steady (32–33 sec.) and 200m fast (27–28 sec.)
6 × 300m, split 150m steady and 150m sprint
4 × 600m, split 400m steady and 200m fast

Further sessions for 5000m/10,000m runners:
6 × 800m, split 600m steady and 200m fast
4 × 1200m, split 800m steady and 400m fast.

The athlete should aim to run the first section of these repetitions in a relaxed way then change technique to speed up over the second stage. High quality has to be aimed for, so a good recovery is essential.

Tired surges The first part of the repetition is run at a fast pace—a partial recovery jog follows, then the athlete speeds up again.
Typical sessions:
800m/1500m runners
600m fast, 100m jog, 100m sprint; repeat four times with good recovery between.
300m fast, 50m jog, 50m sprint; repeat four times with good recovery between.
1500m runners
800m at race pace, 100m jog, 200m fast; repeat three or four times with good recovery between.
5000m/10,000m runners
1200m at race pace, 100m jog, 400m fast; repeat three or four times with good recovery between.
600m fast, 50m jog, 200m sprint; repeat between four and six times with good recovery between.

Pace injection Here the first part of the repetition is 'cruised', the middle part is surged, and the athlete eases back into 'cruising' pace for the final part. Typical sessions:
800m/1500m runners
6 × 450m divided up 150m cruising, 150m sprint, 150m cruising; 3–4min. recovery jog between each repetition.
4×600m divided up 200m cruising, 200m fast, 200m cruising; 3–4 min. recovery between each repetition.
5000m/10,000m runners
4 × 1200m divided up 400m at race pace, 400m faster by about 4–5 sec., 400m back again to race pace; a good recovery of approximately 4–5 min. will be needed between each repetition.

Pace-injections are particularly valuable to 5000m/10,000m runners and accustom the athlete to incurring a small oxygen debt after the middle surge and recovering during the third stage of each run.

Pace increasers As the name implies, the pace increases as each repetition progresses and some typical sessions could be:
800m/1500m runners
6 × 300m with each 100m of each repetition being a little faster than the one before; 3–4 min. recovery between each.
4 × 600m, each 200m of each repetition slightly faster than the one before; 4–5 min. recovery between each.
5000m/10,000m runners
4 × 1200m, each 400m getting slightly faster; 4–5 min. recovery between each repetition.
6 × 900m, each 300m slightly faster than the one before; 4–5 min. recovery between each repetition.

'Surges' Some typical sessions describe this type of training:
800m/1500m runners
200m fast, 100m jog, 100m fast, 50m jog, 50m fast; repeat five or six times with 300m jog between each repetition.
100m fast, 100m jog, 50m fast, 50m jog, 100m fast, 50m jog, 50m fast; repeat five or six times with 300m jog between each repetition.
5000m/10,000m runners
400m fast, 100m jog, 300m fast, 100m jog, 200m fast, 50m jog, 50m fast; repeat three or four times with 300m jog between each repetition.
300m fast, 100m jog, 200m fast, 50m jog, 200m fast, 50m jog, 100m fast; repeat four or five times with 300m jog between each repetition.

Time trials Time trials used to be a very popular form of training but are not used so often nowadays. They can either be all-out efforts or trials aimed at achieving a target time.

All-out trials are usually run over a distance slightly

shorter than an athlete's chosen racing distance, and can be extremely useful if a runner is having difficulties in finding good class races. It can be informative for an athlete to have an all-out trial before an important race at the start of the competition season, and such a trial will validate the effectiveness of his training or can pinpoint any weaknesses. Some suggested distances (apart from the normal racing distances) are:

> 800m: 600m and 1000m
> 1500m: 1000m and 1200m
> 5000m: 2000m and 3000m
> 10,000m: 3000m and 6000m

The 'flat-out' trial can give a great psychological boost to the athlete if he achieves a good result, but it can be rather demoralizing if a poor time is recorded—particularly if an important race is imminent. Bearing these factors in mind, the following points should be considered when arranging such a time trial:

(a) the athlete must want to do the trial
(b) the coach must be pretty sure that the athlete will achieve a good result
(c) conditions (track, weather, etc.) should be favourable to the athlete recording a good time
(d) if other athletes assist they must be experienced enough to set the right pace and must also not hinder the time-trialist by getting in his way. It must be made quite clear to them that they are there to help the trialist—not to try to beat him.

The trial should be held at least 14 days before an important race. This allows the athlete time to alter his training programme if this is felt necessary.

When the trial has been held the coach must be analytical and give an honest appraisal of the result. He must not be afraid to tell the athlete if the result is disappointing and, should this happen, he ought to be able to find a reason for the poor result and be ready with ways of making improvement.

Although the author is not really keen on time-trials, if he were to use this form of training he would rather choose the type of trial where an athlete sets out to achieve a certain time. Some points to bear in mind with this type of trial are:

1. The target time should be difficult but within the athlete's capability. It is much better for the athlete to achieve the target time and be able to say, 'I still had something in reserve', than for him to fall short of a really difficult time. Such a trial would only be attempted when an athlete was happy with the progress of his training and a good result is almost a foregone conclusion, i.e. confirmation of the 'good vibration' his training is sending him. He should look forward to the time-trial and not be over-apprehensive—rather like the scholar who approaches an examination in the knowledge that he knows the questions he is going to be asked and is ready with the answers.

2. The runner should be told that the trial is not only a test of fitness but is also a guide to the future direction of this training. A 10,000m runner who attempts a level pace 5000m as a trial and finds that he fades badly over the last 1000m is probably short of high-quality aerobic work. A 1500m runner might complete a 1000m trial in the target time but may say, 'I could have kept that pace up for another 500m but could not have speeded up at all'. This runner would probably benefit from more high-quality anaerobic work or race-practice training.

3. Some athletes respond well to time-trials and will perform as well as they would in a competition, while other athletes find that the situation is not exciting enough to bring out their best. The coach must be aware of such factors when analysing the lessons of the trial.

Planning the training programme

So far the various ingredients that go into the 'training-cake' have been discussed, but it is getting the right balance of these ingredients that makes the successful recipe. However, because individual athletes vary so much in their physiological, anatomical and psychological make-up, there is no one standard recipe that will suit everyone. The ingredients remain the same but the mixture varies according to an athlete's strengths and weaknesses. So it is up to each athlete to consider the factors needed to bring about improvement and to relate these to his own requirements and circumstances. If we examined the training programmes of the top 50 athletes in the world at 1500m we would find 50 different schedules. It is therefore impossible to formulate training schedules that will benefit everyone to the same degree, but the intention is to outline a typical year for an imaginary athlete in each event; readers should use this as a guide to plan their own programmes.

The programmes assume that the athletes involved are senior athletes with at least two years' training behind them and have achieved the following results:

> 800m: 1 min. 56 sec.
> 1500m: 4 min. 4 sec.
> 5000m: 14 min. 30 sec.
> 10,000m: 31 min.

The athletes coached by the author all follow the same broad programme, i.e.

1. An *autumn/winter* period which consists mainly of aerobic work but includes some technique and speed-work. A small amount of anaerobic work is included and it is also borne in mind that competing in cross-country races will mean using both the aerobic and anaerobic energy processes.

2. A *spring/early summer* pre-competition period of varied training, aerobic, anaerobic, strength, speed technique and race-practice.

3. A *competition period* during which the training is

used to hold, or slightly improve the athlete's fitness level, but it is the races which actually bring out the best in an athlete.

Athletes should note that the distances quoted in the various schedules are 'close approximates' and need not be absolutely spot-on. When a six-mile steady run is suggested, no damage is done if it turns out to be $5\frac{1}{2}$ or $6\frac{1}{2}$ miles, and if repetitions around a 1500m circuit are indicated then it is quite acceptable if the actual distance is anywhere between 1300m and 1700m. As long as the athlete achieves the desired effect from

Alberto Cova has gained World, European and Olympic 10,000m titles.

the session then the distances used need not be strictly accurate.

Runners will see that 'easy days' are included in all the schedules and it is up to the runner to ensure that these days really are easy days, i.e. days which allow the body to recuperate and adapt to the demands of training. Athletes should not feel guilty on these days; in fact their discreet inclusion is a vital part of any well balanced training programme.

In addition to the physical improvements that come about as a result of constant and intelligent training, there are also the good psychological effects that accrue from the athlete's awareness of his improved physical condition. The runner finds himself handling training sessions with greater ease than previously: he finds himself aiming for times that previously he may have thought beyond him and he becomes aware that he can handle greater training workloads. These are the good feelings that a runner needs behind him to generate the confidence to take on opponents in races. He can do nothing about his rivals' levels of fitness but he is the master of his own state of preparation, and being satisfied with his training is the foundation of pre-race confidence.

Fernando Mamede of Portugal holds the 10,000m world record but struggles in competition.

First phase, autumn/winter

This phase, which commences in October and continues until mid-March, starts lightly and builds up to a peak load in February, before easing off a little prior to the beginning of the second phase. Athletes commence this period with one steady-pace run each day of approximately 4–6 miles then after three or four weeks would move into the following schedules. These imaginary athletes are also assumed to have:

(a) Enough time to train twice each day if required. Most serious runners can find the time to fit in two sessions a day if they are really determined to produce results, even though this may mean getting up early in order to fit in a morning session, or sacrificing a portion of the lunch hour.

(b) An all-weather training track within reasonable distance.

800m/1500m schedules (personal bests of 1 min. 56 sec. or 4 min. 4 sec.)

Sunday morning, 8–10 mile steady-paced run
afternoon, 25–30 min. Fartlek
Monday morning, 5 mile easy run
afternoon, 6 mile steady run
Tuesday morning, 5 mile steady run
afternoon, 6 mile run, split 4 miles fast, 1 mile easy, 1 mile fast.
Wednesday morning, 5 mile easy run
afternoon, 4/6 × 1500m or 1 mile at approximately cross-country racing pace with 1–1½ min. recovery between each. Pulse rates can be used to gauge the pace of the run and there should be approximately 160 beats per minute at the end of each fast run, dropping to 130 beats per minute after the recovery period.
Thursday morning, 5 mile steady run
afternoon, 6 mile steady run
Friday, easy recuperation day: either rest or just very easy run for 15 min. or 20/30 min. mobility exercises
Saturday morning, 5 mile steady run
afternoon, 6–8 × 800m/1000m round a hilly grass circuit at slightly faster than cross-country racing pace with 30–45 sec. recovery between each. High and low pulse rates would probably be about 170 and 140 beats per minute. After 20–30 min. rest this session would be followed by 15–20 min. of mobility exercises then a

series of sprint-drills consisting of:

3 × 60m easy fast stride

3 × 60m emphasizing high knee lift

3 × 60m emphasizing very short, very fast strides

3 × 60m easy strides

6 × 60m bounding

3 × 60m acceleration run, i.e. starting slowly and gradually speeding up.

Mobility exercises should be carried out at least three or four times each week. Once every three weeks a 5–6 mile cross country or road race would take the place of the Saturday afternoon session, in which case the sprint drills session would be carried out on one of the other days.

The balance of this programme would be maintained throughout the first phase but progression would be made by:

(a) increasing the distance of some of the steady-state runs

(b) increasing the pace of some of the shorter steady-state runs

(c) increasing the pace of the fast runs in the repetition sessions

(d) towards the end of the phase, starting to include some 60m sprints in the Saturday afternoon sessions.

If the runner were keen to achieve improved results in the major cross-country races which occur in the period mid-February to mid-March, then from January onwards one of the evening steady runs should be replaced with a session of hill-runs; 6–8 runs up a fairly shallow hill approximately 500–600m long, with a quick jog down between each repetition, are suggested. The hill should be steep enough to make the runners lift their knees a little higher than normal. Athletes should remember that they are using this session to gain leg-strength, so attention should be paid to maintaining a normal stride-length and not allowing the knees to turn out. The emphasis should not be placed on the speed of the uphill runs, otherwise the athlete will end up taking short quick strides, but it is inevitable that the repetitions will get faster as the athlete becomes stronger.

The whole winter phase will last approximately 20–22 weeks and should be followed by a week of easy relaxed running. During the phase two further weeks of light relaxed training at seven week intervals are suggested to allow for recuperation and adaptation, and during these weeks the distances covered in the steady runs would be reduced to about 50–60% and the repetition session would also be made easier. It is better to plan for the inclusion of these 'easy' weeks from the beginning rather than to be forced into their inclusion because the athletes feel badly in need of a break.

5000m/10,000m schedules (personal bests of 14 min. 30 sec. and 31 min.)

Sunday morning, 10–15 miles easy run
afternoon, 30–45 min. Fartlek
Monday morning, 5–6 miles easy run
afternoon, 7–8 miles steady run
Tuesday morning, 5–6 miles steady run
afternoon, 6–8 × 1500m or 1 mile at cross-country racing pace with 1–1½ min. recovery between each. Use a similar pulse-rate criterion as the 800–1500m runner to judge pace and recovery time. This session should be alternated on a weekly basis with 4 × 3000m or 2 miles at cross-country racing pace with 1½–2 min. recovery between each.
Wednesday morning, 5 miles easy run
afternoon, 10 miles steady run
Thursday morning, 5–6 miles steady run
afternoon, 6–8 miles run fairly steady but gradually increasing pace over the last 1–1½ miles
Friday morning, 5 miles easy
afternoon, 20–30 min. of mobility exercises
Saturday morning, 6–8 miles steady run
afternoon, 6–8 × 800/1000m round a hilly grass circuit at slightly faster than cross-country racing pace with 30–45 sec. recovery between each. After 20–30 min. rest, follow this session with mobility exercises and sprint drills similar to the 800m/1500m runner.

Mobility exercises are just as important to the longer distance runner as they are to the 800m/1500m runner, perhaps even more so in view of the 'stiffening' effect of the extra distances that they cover.

5000m/10,000m runners will obviously expect to race well at cross-country and road races, so a 5–7 mile race should also be included every other week until January and a longer race every three weeks in the latter part of the first phase. From the beginning of January onwards, the hill-running session described in the 800m/1500m section should be included, and the remark 'easy weeks' is also applicable to 5000m/10,000m runners.

Progression throughout the period should be on similar lines to that suggested in the 800m/1500m schedules.

Opposite *Earl Jones of the USA was 800m bronze medallist at the Los Angeles Olympics.* **Above** *Said Aouita (Morocco) takes gold in the 1984 Olympic 5000m final.*

take place. It is in this period that training is geared to each individual athlete and great care must be exercised in the choice of training distances, intensity of repetitions and time allowed for recovery. The schedules shown for our imaginary athletes will need to be studied carefully and adapted to suit the needs of each individual.

800m (personal best of 1 min. 56 sec.)

Sunday morning, 6–8 miles steady run

afternoon, 6–8 fast but relaxed strides of 150m with slow walk back between each run

Monday morning, 5 miles steady run

afternoon, 4 × 800/1000m fast round a hilly grass circuit with 4–5 min. recovery between each. Use pulse rates of 180 and 160 beats per minute as guides for pace of the repetitions and time allowed for recovery. During this spring phase progression should be made by speeding up the repetitions which will probably mean extending the recovery time.

Tuesday morning, 5 miles steady run

afternoon, four sets of 3 × 200m in 27/28 sec. with 30 sec. recovery between each 200m and 3–4 min. recovery between each set. Progress by increasing the pace of the 200m stretches while maintaining the 30 sec. recovery. The recovery time between sets may need extending. After a 20–30 min. rest follow this session with mobility exercises and sprint drills.

Wednesday morning, 3 miles easy run

afternoon, 5 miles quite fast run

Thursday morning, 5 miles steady run

afternoon, 6 × 300m (42–43 sec.) with 200m jog in 2 min. for recovery. Progress by speeding up the 300m sections while maintaining recovery at 2 min. After 20–30 min. rest follow this session with either six sprints over 60–80m with slow walk back between each run or six fast runs of 60–80m up a 10–15 degree hill emphasizing good range of movement —slow walk back down between each run.

It can be seen that the main physiological gain during this phase will be that of oxygen uptake, although the schedules also include some anaerobic, strength, speed and technique work. The emphasis during this period is on quantity rather than quality and the success of the phase is measured by the sums of all the sessions rather than on brilliant results achieved in a few individual sessions.

Second phase, spring

This is probably the most difficult phase to plan for and the one that calls for most concentration. The sessions are more varied in content and have a greater range of intensity than the winter phase. During the period the runner prepares for the faster pace and more varied tactics that he will encounter during the summer track races, and it is vital that he arrives at the beginning of the competition season with the bulk of intensive training having been completed. Once the competition period starts it is not reasonable to expect an athlete to race well and also to carry out intensive training. During this spring phase the athlete and his coach must be quick to recognize any weaknesses that exist, as time must be allowed for the training effect of remedial sessions to

Friday morning, 3–4 miles easy run
afternoon, 20–30 min. mobility exercises and easy relaxed strides over 50–60m.
Saturday morning, 5 miles easy run
afternoon, 3 × 600m gradually increasing pace with each 200m, e.g. 30 sec., 28 sec., 26 sec., 6–8 min. recovery between each repetition.
20–30 min. rest then mobility exercises and sprint drills.

Towards the end of this phase the athlete should take part in two or three fairly low-key 1500m or 1000m races.

In addition to the exercise periods listed above, the athlete should be spending 15–20 min. each day doing mobility exercises.

1500m (personal best of 4 min. 4 sec.)
Sunday morning, 8–10 miles steady run
afternoon, 35–40 min. Fartlek
Monday morning, 5 miles easy run
afternoon, six hard runs up a fairly shallow hill approximately 450/

500m long—jog back down quickly between each repetition. Concentrate on normal stride length, knees pointing to the front and good thrust with the feet. Follow this work with six or eight easy fast strides over 100m.
Tuesday morning, 5 miles steady run
afternoon, six sets of 2 × 400m (63–64 sec.) with 45 sec. recovery between each 400m and 2½–3 min. jog recovery between each set. As the spring phase unfolds, progress this session by increasing the pace of the 400m sections, while maintaining the recovery times. After a 20–30 min. rest follow this session with mobility exercises and sprint drills.
Wednesday morning, 5 miles steady run
afternoon, 7–8 miles steady run
Thursday morning, 5 miles easy run
afternoon, 6 × 500m (80–81 sec.) with

200m jog in 2 min. for recovery. Progress by speeding up the time of the 500m sections which may mean slightly lengthening the recovery time. After 20–30 min. next follow the session with either eight to ten runs over 100m, starting off at an easy stride then gradually accelerating to all-out sprinting over the last 20–30m; or 10–12 fast runs up a 10–15 degree slope about 60–80m long emphasizing full range of movement with both legs and arms.

Opposite Fartlek training can be performed in the woods or over other undulating soft ground. **Below** Jarmila Kratochvilova of Czechoslovakia, world record holder at 400m and 800m. **Right** South Africa-born Sydney Maree (now living in the USA) has run the second fastest 1500m of all time.

Friday morning, 6 miles easy run
afternoon, 20–30 min. flexibility exercises
Saturday morning, 5 miles steady run
afternoon, four fast runs around a hilly grass circuit about 800m/1000m long with approximately 1½–2 min. recovery jog between each. Progress by speeding up the fast repetition while maintaining recovery time. After 20–30 min. rest follow the session with mobility exercises and sprint drills.

In addition to the sessions listed the athlete should spend a few minutes each day practising mobility exercises. As this phase progresses the athlete should incorporate in the schedule two reasonably hard 3000m races and a low-key 1500m race.

5000m (personal best of 14 min. 30 sec.)
Sunday morning, 10–12 mile steady run
afternoon, 35–40 min. Fartlek
Monday morning, 6–7 mile steady run
afternoon, 5–6 mile quite fast run
Tuesday morning, 6–7 mile steady run
afternoon, 6 × 800m (2 min. 15 sec./2 min. 16 sec.) with 200m jog recovery in 1½/2 min. between each. As the phase progresses, increase the quantity to 8, gradually reduce the recovery time to 100m jog in 45 sec. while maintaining the pace of the repetition. After 15–20 min. recovery follow this session with 6 × 150m starting each run quite slowly then gradually accelerating to sprinting over the last 20-30m. Walk back slowly between each run.
Wednesday morning, 5–6 mile steady run
afternoon, 8–10 mile steady run
Thursday morning, 6–7 mile steady run
afternoon, two sets of 8 × 400m (64–65 sec.) with 30–45 sec. recovery between each 400m and 2½–3 min. recovery between each set. Progress the session by increasing the quantity to three sets of 6 × 400m, and by increasing the pace of each 400m while maintaining recovery times. After 15–20 min. rest, follow with mobility exercises and 6–8 easy relaxed strides over 60m.

Friday morning, 5–6 mile steady run
afternoon, 25–30 min. Fartlek
Saturday morning, 6–7 mile steady run
afternoon, six fast runs around a hilly grass circuit about 1500m long with 1½–2 min. recovery jog between each. Improve the session by holding recovery times but increasing the speed of the 1500m lengths. After 15–20 min. rest, follow this session with mobility exercises and sprint drills.

Some flexibility exercises should be carried out each day in addition to the sessions mentioned above. It is quite likely that the 5000m athlete will have had several cross-country or road races during the period so should be familiar with a pace only slightly slower than that he will encounter on the track. However, towards the end of the period the athlete should take part in two or three reasonably hard track races over 1500m or 3000m.

10,000m (personal best of 31 min.)
Sunday morning, 10–12 mile steady run
afternoon, 35–40 min. Fartlek
Monday morning, 6–8 mile steady run
afternoon, 5–6 mile fast run
Tuesday morning, 6–8 mile steady run
afternoon, six repetitions around a fairly flat road or cross-country circuit approximately 1500m long at slightly faster than 10,000m race pace with 1 min. jog recovery between each. As this phase progresses increase to eight repetitions then increase the pace. After 15–20 min. rest follow this session with 6 × 150m easy relaxed strides.
Wednesday morning, 5–6 mile easy run
afternoon, 10–12 mile steady run
Thursday morning, 6–8 mile steady run
afternoon, five sets of 5 × 300m (54–55 sec.) with 100m jog in 1 min. between each 300m and 300m jog in 3 min. between sets. Progress this session by increasing the pace of the 300m fast stretches while maintaining the recovery period. Follow the session with 15–20 min. of flexibility exercises.
Friday morning, 5–6 mile easy run
afternoon, 25–30 min. Fartlek
Saturday morning, 6–8 mile steady run

afternoon, use the same session as for the 5000m on page 46.

The 10,000m runner, like the 5000m runner, will take part in several cross-country or road races at the beginning of the phase but towards the end of the period two or three good-quality races at 5000m are recommended.

The schedules suggested for the spring phase do not indicate any rest days or very easy days, but in fact it is suggested that a recuperation day is vital after about nine or ten days of regular training. This day can be one of either complete rest, easy jogging, or easy jogging plus gentle mobility exercises. In addition one 'easy week' in the middle of the phase and another at the end are recommended. In these weeks the quantity and quality of the training are scaled down by about one third so that the athlete has a genuine feeling of 'recharging the batteries'. However, the whole concept of maintaining a training load must be governed by the athlete's own honest appreciation of his daily mental and physical condition. If the athlete genuinely feels that an easy day on a day off would do a lot of good then this should be taken without any feeling of guilt. On occasions, a reluctance to train may indicate the need for some variety in the training and in these instances it would be a good idea to carry out sessions that produce the same physiological effects by different ways, e.g. substitute a Fartlek session for an interval training session or use an alternative distance in a repetition running session.

Competition period

Although the general concept of training during this period is that of maintaining fitness between races, there is still a certain amount of improvement to be made with training. A high proportion of the sessions will be of a holding nature, i.e. trying to maintain good quality in a relaxed way, but there will be some high quality 'race-practice' sessions that help the athlete to 'peak up' physically and mentally to certain of the more important races. During this phase the athlete should not be constantly proving his fitness during training sessions, but these 'race practice' sessions will help to maintain sharpness and concentration without the tensions of actual races. There is an obvious need to lighten the training load immediately prior to a race and, perhaps not quite so obviously, the need to allow the athlete to recover both mentally and physically from the effects of a hard race. So if the athlete is racing every week then there is a minimum of at least three days every week spent in pre-race relaxation, racing then post-race recovery. If the training load is quite light during the other four days then there is a distinct possibility of losing a certain amount of fitness if this weekly racing is maintained for too long. In the author's opinion, the best way of overcoming this difficulty is for an athlete to divide the competition phase into periods of racing actively alternating with periods of 'topping up' training. The suggestion is for racing periods of approximately 20 days interspersed with topping-up periods of approximately 10 days.

The schedules quoted are for athletes who are racing every weekend, but it should be fairly simple for readers to devise a topping-up period based on the sort of work carried out during the spring phase.

The Brazilian Joaquim Cruz: in 1984 he made the closest challenge yet to Coe's 800m world record of 1981, and has made the fastest-ever mile debut.

800m (personal best of 1 min. 56 sec.)

Sunday morning, 5–6 mile easy run
afternoon, 25–30 min. Fartlek
Monday morning, 4–5 mile steady pace
afternoon, race practice—tired surges. 3 × 600m quite fast (90% of race pace), 100m jog, 100m sprint. 10–12 min. rest between each practice. After 20–30 min. rest, follow up with 6 × 100m relaxed strides.
Tuesday morning, 5–6 mile steady run
afternoon, 4 × 300m very fast runs (39–40 sec.) with 7–8 min. rest between each run. After 15–20 min. follow this session with mobility exercises and scaled-down sprint drills (i.e. approximately 60% of winter/spring load).
Wednesday morning, 5–6 mile easy run
afternoon, 3–4 mile fairly fast run
Thursday morning, 4–5 mile steady run
afternoon, 6 × 200m at slightly faster than race pace but done in a smooth and relaxed way. Have 200m recovery jog between each. Follow this up after 10–15 min. rest with 6 × 60m of fast strides.
Friday morning, 2–3 mile easy jog
afternoon, mobility exercises
Saturday morning, either easy jog or exercises
afternoon, race

Rather than race 800m every week, the author prefers the athlete to have a varied programme such as a 1500m race, a 400m race, followed by two 800m races.

1500m (personal best of 4 min. 4 sec.)

Sunday morning, 6–8 mile easy run
afternoon, 25–30 min. Fartlek
Monday morning, 4–5 mile steady run
afternoon, race practice—'split interval'. 4 × 600m run with the first 400m at race pace then the last 200m fast. Have 7–8 min. recovery between each practice. After 10–15 min. rest, follow this session with mobility exercises and reduced sprint drills.
Tuesday morning, 5–6 mile steady run
afternoon, 4 × 500m fast (72–73 sec.) with 5–6 min. recovery jog between each run. After 15–20 min. rest, follow up with

6 × 100m, gradually accelerating strides.
Wednesday morning, 4–5 mile steady run
afternoon, 6–7 mile steady run
Thursday morning, 5–6 mile easy run
afternoon, 6 × 300m with 300m jog between each. Aim to run these 300m stretches in 49–50 sec. in as relaxed a manner as possible. After 15–20 min. rest, follow this up with mobility exercises and 6 × 60m sprint.
Friday morning, 3–4 mile easy jog
afternoon, exercises
Saturday morning, exercises or easy strides over 50–60m.
afternoon, race

To vary the racing programme it is recommended that the 1500m runner should alternate 1500m races with 800m, 1000m or 2000m races.

5000m (personal best of 14 min. 30 sec.)

Sunday morning, 8–10 mile steady run
afternoon, 8 × 200m easy relaxed strides with 200m jogs in 2 min. between each
Monday morning, 5–6 mile steady run
afternoon, 6–8 mile steady run
Tuesday morning, 5–6 mile steady run
afternoon, race practice—pace injection. 4 × 1200m divided up first 400m in 70 sec., second 400m in 66–67 sec., third 400m in 70 sec. Have 400m jog in 4 min. between each practice. After 15–20 min. rest, follow up with mobility exercises and sprint drills.
Wednesday morning, 8–10 mile easy run
afternoon, two sets of 6 × 400m (64–65 sec.) with 1½–2 min. recovery between each set. After 15–20 min. rest, follow up with 6 × 150m relaxed strides.
Thursday morning, 6–8 mile easy run
afternoon, 4–5 mile steady run
Friday morning, 5–6 mile easy run
afternoon, mobility exercises
Saturday morning, 3–4 mile easy jog
afternoon, race

It is recommended that the 5000m runner should alternate 5000m races with 1500m or 3000m races.

10,000m (personal best of 31 min.)

Sunday morning, 10–12 mile easy run
afternoon, 8 × 150m easy relaxed strides with slow 150m jog between.

Monday morning, 6–8 mile steady run
afternoon, 4–5 mile quite fast run
Tuesday morning, 5–6 mile easy run
afternoon, Race practice—'pace increasers'. $4 \times 1200m$ with each 400m being faster than the previous one (e.g. 77 sec., 75 sec., 73 sec., 71 sec.). 400m jog in 4 min. between each practice. Have 15–20 min. rest then follow up with mobility exercises and sprint drills.
Wednesday morning, 7–8 mile steady run
afternoon, $6 \times 1000m$ around a fairly flat grass or woods circuit—at slightly faster than race pace but with just $1–1\frac{1}{2}$ min. recovery between each. After 15–20 min. rest follow with $6 \times 150m$ easy relaxed strides.
Thursday morning, 5–6 mile easy run
afternoon, 7–8 mile steady run
Friday morning, 5–6 mile easy run
afternoon, 3–4 mile easy run including some fast relaxed stretches of 80–100m towards the end of the run
Saturday morning, 3–4 mile jog
afternoon, race

It is not possible to race well every week at the 10,000m distance so it is suggested that the runner should compete in one 10,000m race every four weeks with 1500m, 3000m and 5000m races in the intervening period.

Success during the competition period depends as much on the athlete's mental state as on the athlete's physical condition, so each runner must have full confidence in his/her training. The athlete must be satisfied that the training has been hard but sensible, and that everything has been done to 'strengthen strengths' and 'rectify weaknesses'. With confidence in training will come a desire to race against other runners to prove how good he/she is. But having the fitness and confidence is still not enough—the athlete must race intelligently. So good racing tactics must be adopted in order to take full advantage of an athlete's capabilities.

Eamonn Coghlan of Ireland. **Top** *Shadowed by Graham Williamson;* **Bottom** *World champion at 5000m in the Helsinki World Championships of 1983, as Schildhauer of East Germany comes in second and Martti Vainio third.*

Tactics

'If an Englishman challenges you on the last bend, clench your fists and think of your mother!'—trainer's advice to Charles Kilpatrick just before he set a world record for the half mile of 1 min. 53.2 sec. in 1895.

The 800m

Although the 1500m and the one mile race may be the most glamorous in the eyes of the spectator, the 800m is really the middle-distance race *par excellence*. It is the one race in which the aerobic and anaerobic energy systems are used almost equally and in which just one tactical error can ruin an athlete's chance of success. The two-lap race is now run at such a hectic pace that some physical contact is almost inevitable: it has become the survival of the fittest—not only the most physically and 'racing' fit but also the toughest, most positive and aggressive. The 800m runner must be aware of this and stay alert throughout the race to counter any erratic or clumsy actions by his opponents.

As the race has speeded up over the years, the rule concerning the start has been modified in an effort to even out the 'luck of the draw'. Up to 1949 the 800m (half mile in Britain) started on a straight line, drawn perpendicular to the straight and some 30 or 40 yards from the beginning of the first bend (turn in US), in order to give the runners a chance to sort themselves without mishap. This, of course, created a short finishing straight (stretch in US) and often led to a very fast start and a first lap three or four seconds faster than the final lap. At the Olympic Games at Wembley in 1948, however, in order to provide the long finishing straight common to tracks in the rest of Europe, the start took place at the beginning of the bend and, with 12 runners fighting for position, it became painfully obvious that 12 was too large a number of finalists, and that starting on a straight line at the beginning of the bend was dangerous and unfair. The curved starting line was therefore introduced in 1950, so that 'all runners start the same distance from the finish'.

This rule remains valid for all races longer than 800m, and for the 800m at meetings in which few competitors are concerned, such as international matches between two countries but, in 1972, the IAAF decided to experiment, at important meetings like the Olympic Games and Continental Championships, with running the first 300m of an 800m race in lanes. This, however, was not welcomed by athletes or spectators, since it destroyed the character of the race.

In 1977 the present rule was introduced, wherein only the first bend is run in lanes, and the race regained much of its former character of tactics and tension.

The first bend of an 800m race is run in lanes at most important meetings.

Some coaches seem to take the view that tactics are something rather underhand or, at best, some sort of manoeuvre by which an inferior runner can beat a runner with superior ability. In fact, tactics should be thought of as the way in which you get the best out of yourself rather than the worst out of your opponents. A good definition is 'the means you employ to achieve your aim—either to win or to get a high placing or a personal best performance'. The essential prerequisites for successful racing tactics are excellent physical and mental preparation and a good judgement of pace and distribution of effort. Perfect tactics can only help you to make the best out of what you have. They will not, of themselves, win you the race, but poor tactics can often lose it for you.

Herb Elliott, Olympic Champion and world record

holder for the 1500m in 1960, in a time of 3 min. 35.6 sec., which still stands up well to modern standards, claimed that he rarely went into a race with any

Opposite Mike Hillardt failed to make the Los Angeles Olympic final, but his 1984 best at 1500m would have won him the bronze medal. Below Herb Elliott never lost a 1500m or mile race.

preconceived tactics and considered that some runners worried so much about what might happen that they drained themselves of nervous energy. Sebastian Coe, in a press conference prior to the Moscow Olympics, said that he did not prepare for races with individuals in mind. He is also quoted by David Miller in *Running Free* as saying, 'Fundamen-

tally the 800m is impossible to plan'. Any experienced middle distance runner will agree that it is impossible to foretell just what all the other runners will do and fruitless to try to forecast every possible move. The essential about any pre-race plan is that it should be a simple, overall strategy and that, once it has been decided, it should be put out of mind until the time comes to put it into operation. This is a positive approach and it is far better to go into a race with some definite, if flexible, plan of action than to be indecisive, as it appears Coe was before the Moscow 800m. With the first bend run in lanes, there is no excuse for a runner of Coe's speed not to establish an early position in contact with the leaders and then to stay with the pace until he feels the time ripe to strike.

This is an example of a simple, but effective racing plan. With it should go the reminder of the vital importance of remaining alert throughout the race—of complete concentration so that you are alive to all eventualities and can react swiftly.

The popularly held view that only slow races are tactical ones is a misconception. In fact, all races are tactical. If a runner leads at a fast pace right from the start, he does so (unless he is merely a pacemaker) because he believes this is his best tactical plan. Most runners learn, from experience, that to lead all the way and win is almost impossible in top class competition. From Herb Elliott's own accounts of many of his races, it is evident that he generally did have a simple tactical plan. He might decide to take a very early lead, as he did in the 1960 Olympics, but, even with his undoubted superiority over his rivals, he did not reckon on leading all the way. Steve Cram is a runner in the Elliott mould—strong and determined enough to 'front run' a good deal of the race and fast enough to outsprint anybody in the final straight, but he is too intelligent just to act as pacemaker for his rivals in the very early stages of the race.

Tactical sense is best forged in the fire of competition: nothing can take the place of good racing experience for developing a feeling for the race and a knowledge of one's own capabilities. But there are some tactical situations which occur regularly, and a study of them can help the beginner to avoid making too many mistakes during the learning process. Even the experienced champion can benefit from reminding himself occasionally of these basic rules.

Before the race

The athlete's mental state and his thoughts before a race are essential ingredients of his plan of action. The 'torment' of the last hour or so before an important race can be worse than anything the athlete is likely to experience in the race itself. This should be recognized as something unavoidable and, in fact, as a necessary preliminary to a good performance—the worse you feel, the better you run! To be a winner, the

athlete must acquire the ability to hurt himself and, however good he is, he must acknowledge that some part of the race may hurt so much that there is an almost overwhelming temptation to give up the fight. The mental preparation, during the last hour, is vitally important. It is really a matter of willing yourself strongly to push through the critical period of the race, without the least slackening of effort. It can help to remind oneself that these critical periods actually occupy only a small portion of the race, and an iron determination not to give in to them will invariably result in a fresh surge of energy.

At the start

It is better to start too fast rather than too slowly. It is easier to drop down to your coasting speed than to try to work up to it and, if it looks as if you are going to be in the lead as you come to the end of the first bend, it is not difficult to adjust your pace so as to gain a favourable position, not more than 3–4 metres behind the leader and just off the shoulder of the runner in front of you. However, you should guard against the tendency to ease the pace too abruptly, or else you will find yourself quickly passed and boxed in by several runners. It is best to maintain the pace for a little while and then to ease up very gently. You may move out from the pole position, in order to encourage one or two runners to come through the space you have left but, whatever happens, you must be prepared immediately to quicken your pace again in order to establish the position you want.

A runner drawn in one of the outside lanes should not try to rush to the inside of the track as soon as he is free to break. This often leads to collisions and, in any case, he will be running further than he needs to.

He will run the shortest possible distance if he keeps to a direct line from the position at which he enters the back straight to the pole position at the beginning of the second bend. He should stick to this line as far as possible, aiming to establish his position just before he enters the bend.

During the race

It is still a golden rule to run as close to the inside of the bend as possible, without getting boxed in and losing manoeuvrability. It should never be forgotten that running just one bend in the second lane forces you to cover about 4 metres of extra ground. Although it may sometimes be necessary to run wide, or even to pass, on a bend, these should be rare occurrences and should be attempted only if the entire operation can be completed quickly. Conversely, one should always make an effort to respond to any challenge made on a bend, by increasing the pace just suffi-

Steve Cram has continued Britain's strength in middle-distance events in the 1980s.

ciently to keep the challenger running wide.

Sometimes, towards the end of the final bend, it pays to move out and move up closer to the leader, ready to make your final effort. Again, if you find a runner in front of you on a bend slowing up and letting the leader get away, you will have to pass him quickly in order to re-establish contact.

The sort of strategy used in any race depends, first of all, on the importance of the race, whether it is an early-season race or a preliminary round or an important final, and, secondly, on the runner's state of fitness and his confidence in his ability in relation to that of his opponents. These considerations will determine whether he is going to use 'winning' tactics or 'result' tactics. If a realistic appraisal tells him that he has no hope of winning, his best tactics are to do everything he can to run the race at what he feels to be his own best (that is, fastest possible) pace, hoping to produce his fastest time and yet keep some strength for the final effort. He can use the other runners to help pull him round, if their pace is fast enough, but, if they begin to slow up, he will have to take the lead. In this sort of situation no-one can typecast himself as a front runner or a follower; one must adapt to the situation. The aim must be to run the race as evenly as possible, to avoid any interruption to one's smooth, energy-saving rhythm, at all costs to keep up the effort and the pace when it begins to hurt and yet to keep just a little bit back for an all-out finish.

When using winning tactics, the crucial question is when to take the lead. In preliminary rounds, if nobody else is prepared to establish a fast pace, it is often best to take a very early lead, give yourself an uninterrupted passage and 'stretch' the opposition, so that you are in a very safe position for qualifying by the time you hit the finishing straight. This is far safer, and less tiring, than leaving it to a mad scramble for the last 100–200m. In a final you may have a tactical plan, based upon what you know about the opposition and, perhaps, on the weather conditions, but the ultimate decision depends upon the early pace and the tactics of the other runners. It may be, for instance, that you have planned to start your final effort soon after entering the back straight for the last time, but you find that one or two of your opponents make the break even sooner and at what seems a 'killing' pace. The best plan, in this case, is to go with them, hang on as closely as you can while still keeping relaxed and let them pull you along for a while, until you feel the pace becoming bearable again. That is the time for you to strike—and, once having gained the lead, you must aim to keep it. It is also possible to 'jump' into the lead and give your opponents a psychological knockout and still keep back just a little something to ward off any possible further challenge.

Zamira Zaitseva leading Olga Dvirna and Gabriella Dorio in the 1500m at Helsinki.

Boxed in

This is the situation, beloved of and often over-dramatized by TV commentators, in which an athlete finds himself hemmed in on all sides and unable to control his own pace. There is no easy way out of this situation and no hard and fast rule to cover all eventualities. Prevention is better than cure and good tactical positioning is the best method of prevention. Most of the 'in-fighting' during an 800m takes place in the middle of the pack and it is easier to steer clear of any barging, resulting from abrupt changes of pace or direction, if the athlete stays close to the leader and positions himself in the outer half of the inside lane, 'on the shoulder' of the runner in front of him, so that he is free to move up and answer any challenges that may come from the runners behind him.

In a really fast 800m, however, when every athlete is running close to his limit, occasions will arise when even the finest tactician may find himself boxed in. If it happens in the early stages of the race, there is no great problem. The first essential is to keep a cool head. The sooner the athlete is out of this position the better, but any impulsive effort to get clear may well lead to collisions, which will possibly upset him for the rest of the race. To drop back and then run around five or six runners to recover position is not really feasible in a fast 800m. The only practical plan is to maintain the pace and keep watching for the slightest sign of a space developing, which will enable him to move out into a better position.

Being boxed in during the last 200m, of course, can be disastrous. Yet there are examples of great runners finding themselves in this predicament and still, by remaining resolute and alert, extricating themselves from it. In the 1956 Olympic Games 800m final, Great Britain's Derek Johnson seemed to be in a hopeless position—lying fourth and well boxed in, when within 50m of the finishing line—but a gap appearing in the group of runners in front of him galvanized him into action and his lightning spurt failed only by inches to win him the gold medal. Again, in the Rome Olympics of 1960, Peter Snell looked to be hopelessly boxed in by three runners as he came to the end of the final bend—but he kept his head and seized his only chance of winning by sprinting through a gap on the inside, as the leader Wägli of Switzerland made the fatal mistake of moving out, as he entered the final straight.

Opposite Sebastian Coe in the vest of his new club, shows perfect tactical positioning on the bend.

Below New Zealand's Peter Snell (83) snatches the 800m gold medal from Roger Moens at the 1960 Olympics.

The lesson here is plain—never relax your effort in the slightest until you have crossed the finishing line—however hopeless the position may seem. A lot can happen in the last 100m, when you may find yourself getting stronger as your opponents weaken.

The finish

The cardinal rule is that, once the athlete is committed to his finishing effort, there must be no let up. Looking back in an 800m race can be justified only if it takes place during a preliminary round, in order to preserve energy for the final. Even then, the athlete should guard against the common tendency to ease up during the last one or two metres before the finishing line. Even in his training runs, he should make a habit of keeping up the pace right through to a spot some three or four metres past the line.

1500m (and mile)

The slower tempo of the 1500m makes the race tactically less exacting, but only marginally so, and all that has been said about the 800m still applies to a very large extent, especially during the last lap.

In one sense, the 1500m is a more difficult race; concentration has to be maintained over a longer period and, whereas in the 800m the critical phase generally occurs during the third 200m, in the 1500m it can be extended to most of the third lap. These are the times when the ability to hurt oneself and still retain mental toughness is of paramount importance. Maintenance of racing speed, at a time when fatigue is beginning to make itself felt, implies a progressive increase of effort when the natural tendency is to ease up. Pace judgement is really a matter of learning how to spread one's effort most efficiently throughout the race, and it can be learnt by anyone with a will to do so; it is simply a matter of practice and this does not even have to be carried out at racing speed.

An excellent pace judgement/effort distribution practice is to run 1600m at half effort, aiming to cover each 400m lap in identical times. Even at half effort, the runner will find that he has to push himself quite a lot during the third lap in order to avoid any loss of pace, and this will help to develop the necessary feeling of progressive effort, in order to achieve level pace.

Moreover, since there is invariably no problem with the last lap, this sort of practice helps to give the runner the confident knowledge that the effort and will-power required to master the most punishing part of a race will in no way detract from his ability to make a strong finish.

Willi Wulbeck, Detlef Wagenknecht and Peter Elliott (63) stretch for the tape in an 800m race, and show the importance of maintaining full effort to the finish.

Level-pace running is recognized as the ideal way to run a middle- or long-distance race, but a study of the intermediate times of world record races shows how tactical situations often make this ideal difficult to achieve. Coe's world record of 3 min. 49 sec. for the mile, set in Oslo in 1979, with laps of 57.8, 57.5, 57.7 and 56 sec., was as near the ideal as anyone is likely to get; however, in his 1500m record of 3 min. 32.1 sec., established a month later in Zurich, ideal pace was rendered impossible by Kip Koskei's suicidal first lap of 54.2 sec. (Coe 54.4 sec.). In fact, Coe's pace for the remainder of the race, 59.6 sec., 57.6 sec. and a last 400m of 56.8 sec. (41.2 sec. for the last 300m) was remarkably level under the circumstances.

Lap times, however, do not tell the whole story. They can conceal frequent and abrupt changes of pace during the laps—and these are the real enemies of conservation of energy.

The aim should be to run the least possible distance and, at the same time, to maintain a smooth, unbroken rhythm for as much of the race as possible; the 'jump' pass is a very effective tactical weapon, but it should be reserved for use on just one occasion—as a *coup de grâce* and as the initiation of the final effort.

5000m and 10,000m

Tactics are similar in these two events and most distance runners compete in both with equal success. Much of what has been said about tactics in the 800m and 1500m will often apply during the final lap of these longer races but, for most of the time, the slower pace and much longer duration of the longer races allow the runners much more freedom to run in pole position without fear of being boxed in. In fact one of the most important tactical rules in these events is to keep well in to the inside of the track on all bends; running just 0.5m wider than necessary on every bend in a 5000m race would mean covering about 50m extra ground.

Basically there are three types of distance runner:
(a) those who are capable of excellent times but who lack a really fast finish in the last lap
(b) those who are capable of excellent times and who can also, if necessary, produce a brilliant turn of speed during the last lap or the last 200m
(c) a select group of true 'front runners', like Kuts, Bedford and Clarke, whose enormous talent encourages them, and accustoms them, to get out in front very early in the race and break clean away from their opponents; they are quite happy breaking world records like this but sometimes fail to achieve their aim to win, when one or two runners refuse to be shaken off.

Opposite *Ron Clarke (102) leads from Mohamed Cammoudi in the 1968 Olympic 5000m.* **Left** *Dave Bedford—former 10,000m world record holder.*

The first group have to rely upon a fast pace right from the start; if necessary they will have to take the lead themselves to make it so, but it will be better for their final result if they do not have to do this too early in the race. They will certainly have to rely upon a long finishing effort, maybe starting it as early as three laps from the finish, as did the New Zealander, Murray Halberg, in some of his best runs.

The second group will normally be content to follow the pace until they feel ready to attack. The timing of their attack will depend upon their feeling within themselves and upon the way the race has progressed. It may come very early, as when Lasse Viren started his final effort 3000m from the finish in the Olympic 10,000m at Munich in 1972, or it may come as late as the last 200m, as happened in Viren's win in the 5000m at the same Games.

The distance runner who aims to achieve world class times, and to win the big races, cannot afford to be typecast as a front runner or a follower; he must be either when it is right to be so. Dave Moorcroft showed how a recognized follower and fast finisher can also possess the endurance, determination and confidence to take the lead in a 5000m race shortly after the completion of a very fast first 1000m, then maintain an extremely level pace, fast enough to outdistance some of the world's best 5000m runners, and still show good acceleration over the last 400m.

The third group, in a way, have their tactics imposed upon them by their own nature and great ability. If they can make a clean break, they have no problem in winning their races but, when in the really big races like the Olympic finals they sometimes find this impossible to do, they would do well to modify their tactics, persuade somebody else to take the lead while they have a little breather for a lap or two somewhere in the fourth kilometre, and then make a really determined, long drive for the finish.

Opposite *Dave Moorcroft (337) splashes round a wet Athens track in 1981 shadowed by Thomas Wessinghage.* **Above** *Henry Rono, simultaneous holder of the 3000m, 3000m steeplechase, 5000m and 10,000m world records in 1978.*

	SOME 5000m WORLD RECORDS				
	Intermediate 1000m times				
	1	2	3	4	5
Zatopek 1954 13 min. 57.2 sec.	2 min. 43 sec.	2 min. 47 sec.	2 min. 49 sec.	2 min. 52 sec.	2 min. 46.2 sec.
Kuts 1957 13 min. 35 sec.	2 min. 37.8 sec.	2 min. 46.5 sec.	2 min. 44.4 sec.	2 min. 44.2 sec.	2 min. 42.1 sec.
Clarke 1966 13 min. 16.6 sec.	2 min. 40.2 sec.	2 min. 36.2 sec.	2 min. 41 sec.	2 min. 41.6 sec.	2 min. 37.6 sec.
Viren 1974 13 min. 16.4 sec.	2 min. 40.2 sec.	2 min. 40.2 sec.	2 min. 41 sec.	2 min. 41.2 sec.	2 min. 33.8 sec.
Rono 1978 13 min. 08.4 sec.	2 min. 42 sec.	2 min. 36 sec.	2 min. 37.2 sec.	2 min. 39.3 sec.	2 min. 33.9 sec.
Moorcroft 1982 13 min. 00.42 sec.	2 min. 37.6 sec.	2 min. 35 sec.	2 min. 37.4 sec.	2 min. 38.7 sec.	2 min. 31.7 sec.

SOME 10,000m WORLD RECORDS
Intermediate 1000m times

	Zatopek 1954	Kuts 1956	Clarke 1965	Viren 1972	Bedford 1973	Rono 1978
1	2 min. 47.5 sec.	2 min. 42.5 sec.	2 min. 41.5 sec.	2 min. 36.9 sec.	2 min. 40 sec.	2 min. 47.5 sec.
2	2 min. 56.7 sec.	2 min. 51.5 sec.	2 min. 43.5 sec.	2 min. 41.9 sec.	2 min. 43.2 sec.	2 min. 42.7 sec.
3	2 min. 54.0 sec.	2 min. 51.0 sec.	2 min. 46.0 sec.	2 min. 47.6 sec.	2 min. 45.2 sec.	2 min. 43.4 sec.
4	2 min. 55.8 sec.	2 min. 54.6 sec.	2 min. 47.0 sec.	2 min. 49.2 sec.	2 min. 46.2 sec.	2 min. 51.0 sec.
5	2 min. 53.6 sec.	2 min. 49.0 sec.	2 min. 47.0 sec.	2 min. 48.3 sec.	2 min. 44.8 sec.	2 min. 44.4 sec.
6	2 min. 55.4 sec.	2 min. 53.4 sec.	2 min. 48.0 sec.	2 min. 51.9 sec.	2 min. 46.8 sec.	2 min. 46.7 sec.
7	2 min. 53.4 sec.	2 min. 52.0 sec.	2 min. 50.0 sec.	2 min. 52.0 sec.	2 min. 48.0 sec.	2 min. 44.3 sec.
8	2 min. 55.2 sec.	2 min. 53.5 sec.	2 min. 50.0 sec.	2 min. 50.0 sec.	2 min. 47.8 sec.	2 min. 42.1 sec.
9	2 min. 55.8 sec.	2 min. 55.0 sec.	2 min. 46.0 sec.	2 min. 51.4 sec.	2 min. 48.4 sec.	2 min. 43.4 sec.
10	2 min. 46.8 sec.	2 min. 47.9 sec.	2 min. 40.4 sec.	2 min. 29.2 sec.	2 min. 40.4 sec.	2 min. 37.0 sec.
	28 min. 54.2 sec.	28 min. 30.4 sec.	27 min. 39.4 sec.	27 min. 38.4 sec.	27 min. 30.8 sec.	27 min. 22.5 sec.

Lasse Viren trails Mohamed Kedir with Miruts Yifter (both of Ethiopia) third in the final of the 10,000m at the Moscow Olympics.

Tactics in the 5000m and 10,000m races are very closely linked with judgement of pace and effort —whether to follow or lead, when to take the lead, where to make the final effort, whether to maintain a close or fairly loose contact—all these decisions are based on the feeling for pace and effort, which is developed through intelligent training and racing.

A study of intermediate times shows a 'classic' pattern, common to all middle- and long-distance races. Taking sectors of 200m for the 800m race, 400m for the 1500m race and 400m or 1000m for the 5000m and 10,000m races, the classic pattern is for a first sector slightly faster than the average pace, middle sectors below the average pace, and getting progressively slower, and a final sector again faster than average pace.

There have been, of course, some notable exceptions to this rule. In 1966, Jim Ryun ran a world record mile of 3 min. 51.3 sec., with laps of 57.1, 58.1, 59.6 and 56.3 sec.—the classic pattern—but, the following year, he set a new record of 3 min. 51.1 sec. with an astonishing sequence of 59.0, 59.9, 59.7 and 52.5 sec!

A study of the intermediate times given in the Tables on pages 65 and 66 shows that this pattern seems to be the 'natural' one for the long distances. There is a 'natural' tendency for the pace to slacken after the first few laps and then to pick up again in the last lap or so. However, the fact that this 'classic'

Top *Emil Zatopek being supported by team-mates and Yugoslavian team members having won the 1948 Olympic 10,000m in London, and* **Inset** *He loosens up at the same games.* **Opposite** *Jim Ryun, while being world record holder, was unable to take the gold at 1500m in the Mexico Olympics.*

Mary Decker's intermediate times
World Championships, Helsinki, 1983

1500m

400m	800m	1200m	1500m	Last 400m
64.04 sec.	2 min. 10.92 sec.	3 min. 16.67 sec.	4 min. 00.9 sec.	
64.04 sec.	66.88 sec.	65.75 sec.	44.23 sec.	60.02 sec.

3000m

1000m	2000m	3000m
2 min. 51 sec.	5 min. 48.19 sec.	8 min. 34.62 sec.
2 min. 51 sec.	2 min. 57.19 sec.	2 min. 56.43 sec.

pattern occurs in so many world record runs should not be taken to indicate that this should be the runner's aim—that would be to confuse aim with achievement. Good distance runners do not aim, or wish, for a progressive loss of speed during the greater part of the race; in fact, their great efforts to prevent this happening often limit such time losses to a bare minimum.

Level-pace running is the most efficient but certainly not the easiest or most natural method. A dead level pace, during a long-distance run, can become monotonous, deadening and a nervous strain. Many runners develop a rhythmic pattern, especially when leading, which involves a regular lifting of the pace—a form of progressive increase of effort. What seems like a series of accelerations may, in fact, be both a means of checking a loss of pace and a necessary relief from the grinding monotony of fast, level-pace running.

This is not to be confused with the ultra-fast tactical bursts, used by Zatopek and Kuts, to break contact. It is better illustrated by the superb front running of Mary Decker, which crushes her opponents by its sheer inexorable, unabating pace and yet does not inhibit a brilliant, fast, fighting finish.

In the last decade, coincident with increased social approval throughout much of the world for women's participation in competitive sport, and with the upsurge of interest and participation in aerobic activities, women's middle- and long-distance running has taken a giant leap forward. Mary Decker's split times, in her World Championship races in Helsinki (see opposite), show how close women have come to the men's methods and performances. No doubt, with ever-increasing participation and a more enlightened attitude towards physical education and sport for schoolgirls in many countries, the standard of women's middle- and long-distance running will continue to improve at a faster rate than that of the men for some time to come.

Opposite *Mary Decker, the eventual winner, leads Tatyana Kazankina and Wendy Sly (188) in the 3000m final at Helsinki in 1983.* **Right** *Barefoot Zola Budd (151) and Mary Decker in the 1984 Olympic 3000m final, shortly before the much-publicized incident when Mary Decker caught on Zola Budd's heel—a controversial incident that illustrates the importance of keeping a reasonable distance between athletes on the track, tactically both athletes being in error, Budd for cutting in too soon and Decker for not gently distancing herself with a fending hand.*

A

B

D

E

C

F

Technique

An efficient running action consists of movements which are quite natural, and yet which conform to the mechanical laws of motion, within the limitations of the athlete's physique, strength, suppleness, muscular elasticity and neuro-muscular co ordination. The variations in the running actions of athletes competing in the same event are due to individual differences in these qualities and abilities, which impart to each athlete his own style of movement. Figs 1, 2 and 3 reveal those differences of action, which are mostly due to the varying demands of different events—the demand for power in the sprints and for conservation of energy in the long distances.

The basic running action is formed somewhere between the ages of 2 and about 8. Many youngsters have a naturally almost faultless action, which only awaits maturity and the strength and skill, that will come from many miles of running, to reach perfection (photographs of Sebastian Coe at the age of 13 reveal a running action very little different from that shown in the sequences).

The golden rule should be 'keep it simple!' Too much emphasis on details merely makes over-conscious and clumsy what should be instinctive and natural.

Youngsters should be taught, at a very young age, to 'run straight', to relax the neck, shoulders and hands, to aim for smooth continuity, rhythm and freedom of movement of the legs, to rest the arms and let them move with the legs in an easy relaxed manner for the endurance runs, but to use them with greater range and force, while still retaining a good measure of relaxation, in order to 'urge on' the legs when real speed is required at the finish. A good sprinting arm action is somewhat artificial and , therefore, needs to be consciously acquired, and it does require adequate strength. Because of this, it is capable of improvement throughout the athlete's career.

Fig. 1. Here Cameron Sharp demonstrates the technique of the sprint action as distinct from the middle-distance running action. In photo A the high kick-up of the heel allows the recovery leg to act as a short lever, providing a speedy movement. The heel of the supporting leg generally touches lightly. In photo B the recovery leg folds more and the range of arm action is far greater. In photo C, the arm action is much more forceful than is evident in the middle-distance action. In photos D and E, the back leg folds up quickly and the front foot is in a good position for a powerful backward drive. In photo F, the landing action is shown to be close to a spot below the runner's centre of gravity.

A

B

D

E

C

F

Sequence A

A high kick-up of the heel is mechanically sound, allowing the recovery leg to be brought through as a short lever—providing a speedy movement, in the case of the sprints, or an energy-saving one for the long distances. Assuming good relaxation on the part of the athlete, the height of the kick-up will increase in proportion with the force applied. The heel of the supporting leg is firmly on the ground in the case of the long-distance action; it generally touches lightly in the case of the sprints. There is little variation in the arm action to be seen in this phase.

Sequence B

The recovery leg folds up much more and the range of the arm action is far greater in the sprint sequence.

Sequence C

There is a much more forceful arm action, and the driving leg sweeps back further, in the sprinting action.

Sequences D and E

The arm action is much quieter in the distance events. In the sprint event, the back leg folds up more quickly and the front foot is in a good position for a forceful backward drive. In the distance race it is positioned more for smooth continuity and a more restful transition into the driving phase.

Sequence F

The landing is made much higher up on the sole of the foot in the sprint event and closer to a spot below the runner's centre of gravity.

Fig. 2. Sebastian Coe demonstrates a classic middle-distance running action. The landing position (A) is flat-footed but light, and B and C show a full drive off the ball of the foot. Photo D shows a full rear-leg extension and a range of leg movement that can only come from good flexibility in the hips. Seb's arms are carried correctly (relaxed) and the head remains steady.

A

B

D

E

C

F

Fig. 3. Here Henry Rono illustrates an ideal action for the longer middle-distance events. The heel kick-up (A and B) provides an energy-saving movement as the recovery leg can then swing through for the next stride. The heel of the supporting leg is firmly on the ground. However, in photo B the kick-up is less pronounced than in the sprint action. The arm action for the longer events is much quieter (D and E). The front foot is positioned for smooth continuity and a more restful transition to the driving phase.

Cross-country running

Cross-country racing originated, like many other modern international sports, in the English public school system. References can be found, dating back to the 16th century, to schoolboys taking part in the pastime of 'Hare and Hounds', 'Fox and Hounds' or 'Paper Chasing' and this form of cross-country running was probably quite common much earlier than this. The first recorded cross-country race as such, however, was the 'Crick Run', founded in 1833 at Rugby School. Other schools soon followed suit but another 30 years passed before the new sport was taken up by senior sportsmen.

The laying of an early Hare and Hounds trail (paperchase) startles two passers-by as they take a walk in the woods.

The Grasmere Guides Race in 1901, set in the glorious scenery of the Lake District.

We are told by Walter Rye, in the *Badminton Library of Sports and Pastimes*, that the first organized senior cross-country race took place in 1867 over two and a quarter miles of the 'roughest and boggiest part' of Wimbledon Common. Twelve members of the Thames Rowing Club took part in what they called the 'Thames Steeplechase No. 1', with the sole idea of doing something to keep fit for the next rowing season. However, the run proved so popular that it was decided, the following year, to form the Thames Hare and Hounds Club, specifically for the new sport of cross-country racing and 'Paper Chasing'. Very soon, other clubs sprang up, including such famous names as Blackheath Harriers (at first, Peckham AAC), South London Harriers and Birchfield Harriers.

The first attempt at a National Championship took place in Epping Forest in 1876, but it was a failure because all the runners lost their way! The following year, Thames Hare and Hounds Club won the inaugural championship, over a course of eleven and threequarter miles, in Epping Forest.

By the end of the 19th century the sport had become popular throughout Britain and, in 1903, teams from England, Ireland, Scotland and Wales competed in the first International Cross-Country Championship.

The traditional cross-country course, in Britain, was one of from ten to twelve miles of very varied country, with plenty of hills and heavy going, such as ploughed land, and a fair number of obstacles, such as ditches, streams, hedges, fences and gates, to break up the running rhythm—very unlike many modern championship courses, which are often tailored to suit the spectators rather than the genuine cross-country runners.

Women entered the cross-country arena in the late 1920s. The first English Women's Cross-Country Championship took place in 1927 and the first women's international, with teams from England, France and Belgium, was held at Douai in France in 1933, but a regular programme of international women's championships did not begin until 1967. In 1973 the International Amateur Athletic Federation (IAAF) took control of the sport and the distances of the IAAF World Cross-Country Championships were standardized at 12,000m for men and 4000m for women.

It is often said that cross-country racing has been the basis for Britain's success in the middle- and long-distance events on the track. This appears to be true, for there is nothing better for developing the qualities of stamina and determination, and the capacity to endure self punishment, that are essential for top performances on the track and country alike. Many middle-distance champions have found a full season or two of cross-country racing, in the early stages of their careers, invaluable in laying down a solid foundation of strength and stamina upon which to build the vital speed/endurance for their track events, but most top middle-distance runners nowadays avoid much serious racing over the country.

Cross-country racing, in fact, is very much a sport in its own right. The top championship runners are often outstanding men or women track distance runners or marathoners, but there are thousands of club cross-country runners who find the challenge, variety and cameraderie of cross-country running sufficient to make it their number one sport.

Track athletics is very much an individual sport and, at the very top, so too is cross-country and road racing, but it is possible for the great majority of cross-country runners to share the best of two worlds —that of an individual sport, in which each athlete is completely self reliant and must himself bear the blame for any weakness or failure, and that of a team sport, in which each team member plays an equally valuable and respected role. It is this team element which keeps the base of the pyramid broad and strong; just being in the team count is sufficient

motivation for thousands of runners, who could not aspire even to make one of the first three places in their club championship.

Top-level cross-country racing has come a long way since those early days. Television and race track courses have made it a spectator sport and sponsorship has vastly increased the number and quality of competitions. The IAAF World Cross-Country Championships of 1984, held at the Meadowlands Race Track, New Jersey, attracted a field of 37 senior national teams, with 238 runners finishing the course; 17 teams contested the women's event and 108 women completed the race. The junior races attracted similar numbers of competitors and the races were watched by 18,000 spectators at the course, while millions viewed them on television.

Cross-country racing is now, indeed, a world-wide sport. In Britain, some may regret the loss of some of the friendly, informal atmosphere of the old inter-club races, and many may resent the foreigners' assaults on the British tradition of real, tough cross-country courses, but it has certainly now become a better structured sport, with cross-country leagues flourishing in all areas, besides club, county, district, area and national championships

Fell and mountain races are a more severe form of cross-country running. This photo shows an early fell race.

Traditionally cross-country courses were run over difficult terrain with natural obstacles such as gates and ditches. Championships today are run over easier ground with artificial barriers. Here Grete Waitz (293) clears a straw bale.

Above *Running over ploughed fields is good strength and endurance training for all events.*

Opposite bottom *Dave Bedford leads the English National Cross-Country Championships at Norwich in March 1971.*

Training

Training for cross-country running is basically the same as for any other type of distance running, whether it is on track or road. Track distance runners, in any case, generally do most of their training on road or country and any variations in training, and also tactics, are due to the environment. The cross-country runner needs to learn to cope with a variety of surfaces and situations, uphill and downhill stretches, heavy, clinging mud, long grass, obstacles such as gates, fences and ditches and the tactical problems of massed starts. However, for most runners first-hand experience of these conditions is confined to weekends; the bulk of the training is carried out on the road and, of course, most cross-country runners also participate in road races.

The most important training principle is that of steady, gradual development. Physical qualities such as strength, speed and stamina, which are built up over a period of many months and years, tend to develop to a higher peak and also to endure longer than when their preparation is rushed. There have been notable apparent exceptions to this rule, of course—examples of precocious talent showing world-class ability and performances as teenagers, but these are very much exceptions and they might have developed into even greater athletes, had they been willing to undertake a longer, more gradual preparation.

To observe this principle of a gradual build-up of strength, stamina, speed, tactical ability and mental toughness, the following guidelines are recommended.

Specialization, that is, really serious training and racing, should not be encouraged before the age of about 15 for girls and 18 for boys. Before this, youngsters will develop more naturally and regularly in an informal environment of all-round participation in track and field events, team and individual games, swimming and gymnastics. Running, of itself, can do no harm to any normally healthy youngster, but it is essential not to 'push' the mileage or intensity too soon. While boys and girls are still developing in growth and maturity, it is wise to emphasize the play element and to regulate carefully the amount and severity of training, along the following lines:

Age	Length of run	Frequency weekly	Variation in distance
12–14	Up to 5000m	Up to 3	1500–5000m
15–17	Up to 10,000m	Up to 4	1500–10,000m
18–20	Up to 20,000m	Up to 7	5000–20,000m

There is no need to worry about the 'overload principle' in order to get improvement. According to this principle, improved performance will come about only when the muscular, circulatory and respiratory systems are subjected to gradually increased training loads but, at this stage, there should be no conscious striving for this. As the training progresses, the increased fitness of the young athletes will itself bring about, quite naturally, a faster, overall pace and this, in turn, will give the runners their first taste of the symptoms of fatigue. If they are going to be any good at all, they will soon learn to 'live with' the feeling of discomfort that results from a faster pace than one has been used to and to ignore it,

so that performance does not suffer. This is a natural form of the 'overload principle'—overload without overstrain.

The training programme may then be gradually built up, over the next four to six weeks, along the following lines:

Day one.   5000m steady.
Day two.   Active rest.
Day three.   3000m Fartlek with hills.
Day four.   Active rest.
Day five.   Active rest.
Day six.   1500m at brisk steady pace, or race.
Day seven.   Active rest.

Girls of 11 and 12 are invariably much more advanced than boys of the same age and, indeed, a great many of them at this age enjoy a combination of a very light build and a good cardio-respiratory development, which is highly suitable for distance running, but which, unfortunately, deserts many of them in later years. There is something to be said for the argument that they should be encouraged to enjoy these advantages to the full while they still have them, but there is no doubt that a great number of these prodigies go through a period of great disappointment and frustration later on, when their body shape alters and they can no longer repeat their earlier successes.

The traditional cross-country club 'pack' method of training is still an excellent way of bringing athletes along in a sensible way, so that they may develop steadily from year to year and be at their racing peak when they reach their physiological/endurance peak.

Under this system, training runs are carried out in 'packs' of runners of the same age group and roughly similar ability. Two of the more experienced runners are put in charge of each 'pack', one acting as the pacemaker and generally simply called the 'pace', and the other taking control of the rear and called the 'whip'. It is the latter's responsibility to keep an eye especially on the less experienced runners and to ensure that the pace is not made too fast for them and yet is not so slow as to be ineffective training. A strict rule must be kept that every runner always stays behind the 'pace' unless given permission by the 'whip'.

By the time the runners are ready for senior competition, they should have become used to training pretty well every day of the week, and, if they seriously intend to reach their potential, they will now introduce one or two double sessions per day into the weekly programme. The training will now be similar to that for the long-distance track men or marathon runners, i.e. a well planned mixture of continuous slow, medium and fast running, interval running (on

Opposite Zola Budd training in Bloemfontein. ***Above and inset***
*Girls and boys compete in cross-country races from a relatively
young age.*

the track, road or country), Fartlek (on the country, in
woods or at the beach, etc.), hill running, hill circuits
and repetition running.

What has been said about diet, rest, sleep and
healthy living habits, of course, applies fully to the
cross-country and road runner. The following
suggestions are more specific.

1. Footwear

The running shoes are the athlete's most expensive
and most important accessory and it would be very
foolish to economize on these at the expense of
quality. It is possible for some runners of an extremely
light build to manage quite well without shoes, as long
as the running surface is not too rough or abrasive, but
the runner of normal build will need something to
protect his feet, ankles, knees and even his spine
from the continual jar of landing on unyielding
surfaces.

The most important point about the shoes worn for
any type of distance running is that they must be a
perfect fit, i.e. the front (toe box) of the shoe should be
broad enough and high enough to allow the toes to

Cross-country racing shoes. Both training shoes and spikes have studded heels.

take up their natural position, without undue pressure on the sides or front, while there should be sufficient support along the mid-side sections and at the rear to prevent any sloppy movement of the foot in the shoe. Most runners find that spiked running shoes are best for racing on courses which contain no road, but, for training on road and country, a shoe with a studded sole and heel is most suitable. It should have good shock-absorbing qualities in the heel and sole, and it should have a raised heel wedge and a flexible mid sole; it is important that the tab at the top of the heel section should be soft, padded and not too high, in order to guard against possible irritation of the Achilles tendon. Top runners will, no doubt, be provided with many pairs of shoes and will wear special, very light ones for racing but, if the ordinary club runner has to make a choice, it is best to opt for comfort and durability rather than lightness.

Some runners believe that it is better to toughen the feet up so that they can do without the extra one or two ounces weight of socks (twice as much when wet). No distance runner gets away entirely from blisters, however careful he may be, and anyone attempting to get his feet used to doing without socks can expect to get a few blisters during the early stages. Most commonly these occur under the big toe and where

the edge of the shoe tends to rub against the side of the foot. The simple, but effective, treatment is to burst the blister with a sterilized needle, press the liquid out with a sterile cloth and then simply cover with an antiseptic plaster.

A really well-fitting shoe is the first defence against blisters and other foot ailments, and this applies also to ordinary footwear, for badly fitting walking shoes will cause abnormalities which will be exaggerated by the stress of long-distance running. However, since some slight sliding movement of the foot within the shoe is unavoidable, many runners use some form of lubricant to lessen the friction, or tape parts of their feet prone to blisters. Lanolin is a very good, natural lubricant extracted from pure undyed lambs' wool; strands of this wool may be wound around the toes to provide a supply of lanolin during a run. At least one famous marathon runner used to get his wife to use this pure wool to knit him special racing socks, which would have to be discarded after one race. Other lubricants such as talcum powder or Vaseline are sometimes used, but none of these remedies is long lasting. Most runners will find that the most effective remedy is to harden up the feet gradually and naturally.

Most long-distance runners, however, do wear

socks. There is no real evidence that any one material is better than another, but it is worth remembering that wool certainly fares better than other materials when wet. It provides better insulation against the cold and retains its softness and resilience better than cotton or man-made fibres. It is essential that the socks have no seams, holes or hard spots of any sort and it goes without saying that they should be freshly washed before each run and discarded when they begin to lose their softness.

2. Clothing

The rigours of winter may breed a race of tough runners, but there is no need to make conditions any harder than they already are. Common sense should dictate the sort of clothing suited to your climate.

The runner does not want to be weighed down by a mass of heavy clothing but he does need to be protected from icy winds and wet. On merely cool days, after a preliminary warm-up in a light tracksuit, a long sleeve shirt, supporter and shorts will be sufficient; in really cold weather, tights can be worn under light tracksuit or wet suit trousers, plus light woollen gloves or mittens, a tracksuit top or sweater, two shirts and a woollen hat or a hood. For racing, a short-sleeved and long-sleeved shirt may be needed plus tights. Some runners suffer a great deal from freezingly cold hands which give a lot of pain when warmth eventually returns, but they find that gloves become uncomfortably warm and heavy after a mile or so. A good tip, in this case, is to cut down a few discarded socks and to wear them as gloves until the hands become warm and then throw them away. For training, a pair of light woollen gloves, with a band of elastic sewn to them, can be worn for a while and then strapped to the wrist.

Warm-up

The warm-up serves two purposes:
1. To improve the athlete's performance during the early stages and
2. To guard against possible injuries.

Cross-country races often take place in very cold weather and they generally start fast, especially, of course, when there is a massed start. An adequate warm-up is essential to allow the runner to get away sufficiently fast to gain a good position, without having to expend too much energy.

Easy running, if necessary warmly clad, is just about the best way to get the circulation and respiratory system functioning satisfactorily and to provide warmth to the muscles, tendons and ligaments. This alone will go a long way towards ensuring good mobility in the joints and a responsive locomotive system, but it is strongly urged that, in addition, ten minutes or so should be spent on exercises to stretch gently the muscles of the calf (Achilles

The start of the English National Cross-Country Championship in the 1970s. Steve Ovett (322) and Brendan Foster (804) show early.

tendon), the front and back of the upper leg, the hips, back and shoulders. If the runner has experienced any muscular or tendon trouble, especially in the case of the Achilles tendon, it is best to carry out these exercises before any running is attempted. Otherwise, a good system is to start with five or ten minutes of very gentle running, then carry out these stretching exercises for ten to fifteen minutes and then conclude the warm-up with about fifteen minutes of slightly faster running.

Tactics

To a large extent, the tactics employed will depend upon a good knowledge of the course. The runner, therefore, should find out all he can about it, either by walking or gently running around it or, if this is not possible, by studying the course plan and directions. It is not sufficient to rely on the course markings; these may seem perfectly clear at walking pace, but the stress and flurry of racing, especially when fatigue is beginning to make itself felt, can easily blunt one's perceptions and lead to errors of judgement and direction. The better you know the course, the better you can judge how to distribute your effort, where to make a break and where to start your final effort.

The start

Inter-club matches generally present no problem at the start, since there are not too many runners and care is normally taken to see that no obstacles or narrow paths are encountered, until the field has had a chance to thin out a little. However, the first 200–300m is often a bit of a rush and the athlete will have to get used to this, but he should guard against continuing this hectic pace for too long. His best tactics are to start off at a brisk pace, with the field, and to let them take him along for a while, trying to relax into his own 'comfortable' racing pace as soon as possible.

However, if he has any ambitions to do well in championship races, he will have to learn to cope with the mad charge for the first 400m or so, which is inevitable under championship conditions, such as at the English Nationals in 1984, when 2000 runners were herded into 250 starting pens and the start line extended over a width of 500m. The first racing technique to master is how to stay within reasonable distance of the leaders during the frantic first 400m and yet conserve as much energy as possible. The principle is still the same—start off fast enough to get a good position among the leading 10 or 20 and then settle, as soon as you can, into your 'coasting' pace.

Strengths and weaknesses

The same qualities of endurance, strength, speed, skill, mental toughness and will to win are found in all good distance runners. It is the proportional differences in this mixture that lead to the variations sometimes found in the specific abilities on the track, on the road or in the country. Some runners are fine on the track and also, often, on the road or on fast parkland, but are not nearly so good when it comes to really heavy going or uphill running. Some find it difficult to cope with the breaks in rhythm caused by the different types of terrain and obstacles. Others seem to thrive on these variations and revel in heavy going. Some are good uphill runners while others are much better on the downhill stretches.

It does not take long for a runner to find out his strong points and his weaknesses. The best policy then is to capitalize on one's advantages but also to work at improving one's failings. If a runner is especially good at downhill running, it makes sense to try to use this ability to make a break or to overtake, and still to try to hang on when the going gets tougher. It is always a good thing to cherish and nurture one's strong points and not to take them for granted, but it is possible to retain them and, at the same time, to improve one's weaknesses.

In this regard, it should be noted that there is often quite a difference between the technique used in racing and that used in training. Racing technique is designed for speed with economy of effort. What you do in training is often aimed at improving qualities

The 1978 World Cross-Country Championships at Glasgow. **Left** *A muddy uphill stretch.* **Above** *John Treacy on his way to victory.*

such as speed, endurance, strength and suppleness and it may, at the time, have little to do with economy of effort. There is often an essential difference between uphill racing technique and work carried out in training to improve uphill running ability. In racing uphill, it pays to lean forward a little and to shorten and quicken the stride slightly. In uphill training runs, however, where the aim is primarily to build up muscular power and local endurance, it will be more effective to keep up and sometimes even lengthen the stride. This will be very wasteful of effort, but is the best way to gain the power necessary to improve uphill racing ability. Bounding exercises up medium slopes have a similar beneficial effect.

Downhill running

Steep slopes are dangerous and should not be included in cross-country races. If they are encountered in training runs, they should be negotiated slowly and carefully. Medium slopes, if the correct technique is employed, provide an excellent opportunity for fast running with real economy of effort. No attempt should be made to stop the natural build-up of speed. In fact, any effort made by the runner to check his momentum will be much more energy-consuming than simply allowing the slope to carry him along. The stride can now be lengthened as well as quickened and the trunk should be kept fairly upright. As long as optimum relaxation is maintained, it will now be possible to run very fast with a minimal expenditure of energy.

Running over difficult terrain

There is only one efficient way of negotiating rough ground or heavy surfaces, such as ploughed fields or muddy patches, and that is to get over it fast. The same applies to short, fairly steep uphill stretches. The sooner you are over them, the less energy you expend, in proportion to your speed. Rough ground should be approached boldly, with some acceleration. A fairly short, quick stride will help both balance and speed and this sort of technique is often most effective in passing or shaking off an opponent.

Obstacles

The same principle applies to the clearing of obstacles. The aim should be, as far as possible, to 'run over' them so that there is the least possible check to one's rhythm. With practice, gates and fences can be cleared economically and quickly by stepping on to a middle bar and then stepping up, over and down in one continuous movement. Whatever the obstacle, it is always best to approach it boldly, without hesitation, and to get over it quickly and smoothly—the technique of the steeplechaser at the waterjump.

During the race

Even-pace running is efficient on level and regular surfaces. The cross-country runner should follow this principle, inasmuch as he should try to prevent any fall-off in the overall speed of the race—on the whole, he should aim for a level distribution of energy. Cross-country, however, and road racing to some extent, lend themselves to advantageous variations of speed and effort. A little extra effort on rough ground, on uphill slopes or in clearing obstacles is tactically effective and can generally be offset by a little more relaxation on the easier running sections. Cross-country and road runners should try to make use of their strong points to 'crack' the opposition, and this will often necessitate a variation of pace and some extra effort. On the other hand, when a runner finds that an opponent is looking strong and the effort to stay with him is becoming increasingly difficult, he should always keep in mind that appearances are often very deceptive. Most likely his opponent is feeling just as bad as he is, and, if his attempt to break contact fails, he will feel much worse! It is surprising how long you can hang on desperately to an opponent and then suddenly find him weakening and yourself getting stronger. The moral is never to over-estimate the condition of the opposition and never to be deceived by the bad time you may be going through into thinking that you have 'had it'.

The finish

Finishing technique is basically the same in any type of distance race. In small inter-club races, the only

Wet muddy conditions typical of some cross-country courses at club level.

extra problem about the finish is knowing how far you have to go to get there! If you are well acquainted with the course there is no problem, but, if it is new to you, then the more you can get to know about the last 1500m or so the better. Without this knowledge it will be impossible to time your finish perfectly.

In big championship or invitation races the position is more difficult because of the complicated nature of the area behind the finish line. There really should be

no difficulty, since the actual finish line is reached long before the rest of the paraphernalia filling up the area behind it, but the perceptions of a tired and excited runner in the final sprint are far from normal. It is wise, therefore, to make a thorough inspection of the finish line and the whole area around and behind it. The most common mistake is to imagine that the finish line is a bit further away than it actually is, and so mistime the final effort.

In big races the finish line is actually very clearly defined and the approach to it will normally be fenced off to keep out spectators. Behind the finish line there will be several roped-off lanes, called chutes, and a number of officials. Each runner will be timed and placed at the finish line and he will then be guided along one of the chutes, in his correct order of finishing, by chute officials. His position will then be recorded at the end of the chute. In important races the runners may wear numbers and also have tags pinned to their singlets containing relevant information such as name, age, sex, team, etc. Sometimes these tags may be used, in conjunction with electronic devices, to give an accurate record of the finishing order.

Road racing

There has been some form of road racing for as long as there have been roads. The earliest evidence we have of a running activity is a representation on Egyptian bas-reliefs dating back to 3500 BC. During the reign of the Pharaohs it was the custom for Egyptian noblemen to employ 'running' footmen to precede their carriages, proclaiming the importance of their masters and clearing the way for them. In Britain, during the 17th century, the gentry also adopted this custom and it became a matter of pride for a gentleman to employ, as his footman, a very fine runner. The craze for betting, among the gentry, soon led to matches being arranged between their footmen and it was not long before professional 'pedestrians' came on the scene. As the popularity of these running matches grew, a few of the gentry were also tempted to show their paces and there emerged from this the birth of the two classes of amateur and professional (similar to the situation of 19th century and modern ultra-distance running).

There are many records of this early type of road racing in Britain. In Burton's *Anatomy of Melancholy*, it is recorded that 'On the 1st December, 1653, a butcher from Croydon covered, in less than an hour and a half, the 20 miles that separate St Albans from London.' According to Walter Thom, in his book *Pedestrianism* published in 1813, the four-minute mile was run long before Sir Roger Bannister set his record. Thom records that, in 1770, 'a pedestrian, for a bet, ran the mile from Charterhouse Wall to Shoreditch Church in four minutes.'

However, road racing really began to be organized as a popular sport with the coming of the first cross-country clubs. As so much of the training was carried out on the roads, it was a natural progression for clubs to organize their own road races, first as club championships and handicap races, and then on an inter-club basis. Inter-city road relay races began to achieve some popularity during the 1920s and 1930s but, until the late 1970s, cross-country racing assumed much greater importance than road racing.

In the 1970s, however, road racing, from being a rather esoteric event hardly noticed by the general public, began to emerge as a major sport. Many factors contributed towards this explosion of interest. The medical profession became much more convinced of the value of aerobic exercise as a precaution against heart disease, and road running presented itself as a simple, cheap and measurable way of achieving a state of 'fitness'. Jogging became fashionable and 'fun runs' introduced an element of enjoyment that attracted millions of non-athletes throughout the world. Television played a major role in this boom. The spectacle of thousands of participants in major marathon races encouraged thousands more to take up the sport and, at the same time, greatly enhanced the prestige of the top runners. The widespread exposure by the media attracted more sponsorship which, in turn, made possible bigger and higher quality competitions.

In the USA especially, road running assumed the stature almost of a cult—books and magazines on running proliferated and what is actually a fairly simple and natural activity donned a mantle of mysticism. But there is no country in the world that has been untouched by the road racing boom; every major city has its own road race and many countries produce quite elaborate handbooks entirely devoted to road racing, the French one, for example, listing more than thirty races each month taking place from March to December.

Technical considerations

The advice on tactics given in the section on cross-country racing applies, to a very large extent, to road racing.

Above Greek bas-relief of an early road race. **Opposite bottom** *Nineteenth century road races were often competitions for wagers.*

Certainly, the importance of well-fitting and well-constructed footwear and the care of the feet cannot be over-emphasized. Similarly, the value of a very gradual build-up must be stressed. Nothing really worthwhile comes easily, of course, although it cannot be denied that the top runners are blessed with a lot of natural ability. It is as well to recognize that success in distance running of any sort does require determination and will-power, and that these qualities will be encouraged by the knowledge of fitness gained by sensible and conscientious training, but it is wrong to imagine that, to be of any value, running training must always be hard and fast. Coaches who talk about training sessions being useless unless the athlete feels thoroughly sick after them, must either have never done any distance running themselves or else be very exceptional people!

It is important for the beginner to realize that the build-up to the sort of training carried out by experienced, top-class runners can be comparatively painless—at least, it is possible to learn to punish yourself and actually enjoy the experience, as long as the process is a gradual one and the types of training

THE TEN-MILE RACE AT LILLIE BRIDGE BETWEEN W. G. GEORGE AND W. CUMMINGS FOR £100 A SIDE

Opposite There are now a vast range of books and magazines to inform the runner. **Above** The start of a road race is usually crowded and fast.

session are well varied, both in content and in effort.

Runners who have some natural ability and are highly motivated feel that it is very necessary to build up the 'mileage'. This is very natural and correct, especially if this build-up takes place over a period of several years, but sheer 'mileage' must not be allowed to take precedence over everything. If it does, then the law of diminishing returns comes into operation, and the extra mileage becomes unproductive or even negative in its effect. Training for road racing, if planned carefully, with good variations in the sorts of course and terrain used, in the distances covered and the pace and effort used for different sessions, can be less monotonous, and therefore more enjoyable than track training. Speed is relative and running, at any distance, contains an element of it; the ability to cope with changes of pace carried out by one's opponents, or initiated by oneself for tactical reasons, is a valuable asset for the distance runner, and a well planned training programme will cater for this capacity and become more enjoyable and motivating for doing so.

Experienced and intelligent runners will invariably discover their own effective and practical training pace over various distances and this will be their own basic pace for most of their steady runs. They may be guided by occasional measurement of pulse counts, but there is little danger of an ambitious athlete running too slowly. He will feel that it is a waste of time running at a pace that will place little stress on his respiration and circulation. He will also feel that there is a place for some proportion of anaerobic work, whatever his racing distance is. It is generally found more enjoyable to train with other runners, but there is certainly a place for solo training, when the athlete can run at a pace that is best for his own training needs at the time, and can use the stopwatch as a guide to the maintenance of the correct effort and to provide some measure of his improvement. This sort of training develops a certain self-discipline in the athlete and this is where the services of a coach to guide, encourage and inform are most valuable. The main advantage is that it is possible to apply a high level of effort in this way, without the sort of nervous strain that often accompanies speed work in the company of other runners.

Organization

Road racing organization is becoming increasingly complicated as the sport gains in stature and popularity. The big annual events now require full-time professional race organizers to ensure safety and fair treatment for the many thousands of runners taking part. Extreme care has to be taken to ensure that courses are measured with accuracy and marked clearly, that proper changing and refreshment facilities are provided, that the whole course is monitored by efficient medical personnel, that adequate provision is made to treat and transport runners who are forced to drop out of the race, and that the arrangements for timing and placing the competitors at the finish will cope with the pressure of high-density races.

The IAAF Development Programme Book No. 4, *Guidelines for the Conduct of Road Racing*, contains a great deal of very useful information of interest to runners as well as race organizers, and is of special significance since it contains the rules governing all international road racing meetings. A summary of the main rules is given below:

1 Distances
The official international racing distances are:
10,000m.
15,000m.
20,000m.
30,000m.
Marathon. (42,165m).

2 Running surface
Races must take place on made-up roads, permissible surfaces being asphalt, concrete, brick and running track (the start and finish may be within an athletic arena). If, through unavoidable circumstances, bicycle paths or footpaths have to be used, they must not exceed 1% of the total race distance. It is recommended that sharp turns, climbs or descents be avoided.

3 Distance and time markers
For distances of 20,000m or less, and in World Championships, Olympic Games, Area Games and World Cup competitions, large distance markers should be displayed every kilometre. In longer road races markers may be displayed every two kilometres or each mile.

The elapsed time shall be called out or displayed every 5 km, or more frequently if possible.

4 Vehicles on course
The race should be traffic-free except for official vehicles. (The relevant police forces should be contacted well in advance and always kept well in the picture—co-operation from them is invariably excellent.)

5 Health and safety
Medical facilities shall be available at the start, along the course at various aid stations, and especially at the finish. Toilets should be available in sufficient quantities at the start, along the course and at the finish.

A competitor must retire from the race if ordered to do so by a member of the medical staff officially appointed and clearly identified by an arm band.

It is forbidden for a runner not in the race, or who has dropped out of the race, to pace another athlete.

6 Water stations and refreshments
Refreshment stations should be located at intervals of 3km/2 miles or less and near the start and finish. Refreshments, which may be either provided by the organizer or by the athlete himself, shall be available at the stations nominated by the competitor.

The organizers shall provide, midway between two refreshment stations, points where water only will be supplied. In warm weather, additional water stations may be provided, equipped with hoses and showers.

7 Course measurement
A course is said to be satisfactorily measured if it is measured with an accuracy of better than one part in one thousand (1/1000). This results in a maximum allowable tolerance of less than 42m at the marathon distance, and less than 10m at the 10,000m distance. It is recommended that 1/1000th of the distance be added to the course to make it slightly longer.

8 The finish
The organization at the finish follows the pattern outlined in the chapter on cross-country racing.

Specialist clubs

There are many specialist clubs throughout the world. In the United Kingdom, the Road Runners Club (Honorary Secretary, Don Turner, 40 Rosedale Road, Stoneleigh, Epsom, Surrey, KT17 2JH), is a very lively organization which publishes a regular newsletter, arranges seminars and provides a special insurance scheme for road runners. Membership is restricted to members of athletic clubs affiliated to the AAA or WAAA. The London Road Runners Club, 6 Upper Montague Street, London W1, has no restrictions on membership and is concerned mainly with the promotion of races in the London area.

Opposite top Avon Cosmetics now sponsor women's road racing around the world. Opposite bottom Road racing in the winter often means the top runners will race in shorts and singlet while slower runners need more protection. While the leaders battle at the front, large groups contest the minor placings at the back of the field (1983 Hogs Back Road Race).

The Marathon

Pheidippides expires after his epic run (drawing by Grosse)

Introduction

There must be many reasons for people wanting to run and finish a marathon. What is surprising is that so *many* people have this desire. In order to examine these reasons we must look back at the history of the event.

History tells us that in 490 BC an Athenian army of around 10,000 soldiers confronted an invading Persian force of at least 80,000 near a town called Marathon, not far from the sea coast, just over 30km across the mountains from Athens. Using superior tactics the Greeks routed the Persians and drove them into the sea losing only 192 men compared with 6400 Persians slaughtered. According to legend, a young soldier named Pheidippides, renowned for his running abilities, was despatched to Athens to convey the good tidings. Although exhausted from the battle Pheidippides set out across the mountains with all possible haste, and on reaching Athens gave to the city fathers the victorious message, 'Rejoice, we conquer.' Having uttered these famous words, Pheidippides fell down dead.

The Greek historian Herodotus, who lived approximately from 484 to 425 BC and was thus contemporary with the Battle of Marathon and able to converse with survivors, makes no mention of a messenger running from Marathon to Athens.

Plutarch, another Greek historian writing more than 500 years later, is the first to mention a messenger from the battle and in doing so ascribes the feat to someone other than a Pheidippides, so this famous run may well be a myth—but what a story!

To return to Herodotus, what he does describe in his history is a run from Athens to Sparta by a professional foot courier named Phillipedes (Pheidippides is very probably a corruption of this name) which was completed in less than 48 hours, a distance of some 150 miles, accomplished over mountainous terrain, and in all likelihood in bare feet. His task was to request the help of the Spartans in repulsing the Persian invaders, but his run was in vain as the Spartans were extremely superstitious and would not march to war until the moon was full, which was several days thence. There is some evidence to

Above *Spiridon Louis, the winner of the marathon at the first modern Olympiad in 1896.* **Inset** *On the occasion of the kindling of the Olympic flame in 1936.*

suggest that Phillipedes returned the next day delivering the reply within 48 hours once more.

Whether legend or history, the story led the Frenchman, Baron Pierre de Coubertin, founder of the modern Olympics, to be persuaded rather reluctantly to include a race from Marathon to Athens in the first modern Olympic games held in Greece in 1896. To the joy of the whole nation this first 'marathon', over a distance of 40km, was won by a Greek shepherd, Spiridon Louis.

Today's standard for the marathon of 26 miles and 385 yards (42km 195m) was set at the measured distance of the 1908 Olympic marathon route between Windsor Castle and the finish at the White City Stadium, Shepherds Bush, London—not the usual finish line for the track races, in fact, but a special finish line in front of the Royal Box.

However, it was not until the Paris Olympics of 1924 that the marathon course was standardized at this rather odd distance, and the intervening Games had differing lengths: 1912 (Stockholm) 40km 200m; and 1920 (Antwerp) 42km 750m.

It is unlikely that the legend of Pheidippides has inspired many runners of the thousands of people world-wide who aspire to the marathon; rather we must look for other deeper reasons for wanting to tackle this daunting race.

The running boom really started in the USA, and as early as 1970 the famous Boston Marathon, which started the year after the inaugural Athens Olympics, had a field of more than 1000. The author was fortunate enough to win this race in a then record time of 2 hr 10 min. 30 sec., but he remembers being amazed by such a host of runners crammed on to the narrow road at the start at Hopkinton, compared with similar races in England where a field of hard-core harrier runners would rarely approach 200.

Main picture Ron Hill training early in the morning.
Inset Derek Clayton leads Ron Clarke in a track race

Returning to Boston in 1975, the field had by then grown to more than 2000. This was doubly amazing as marathon running in England was still at a standstill. Many people attributed the spectacular mushrooming in marathons in the USA to Frank Shorter's victory in the 1972 Munich Olympics, and this may well have been a significant factor. However, as a nation, Americans were perhaps ready for a reaction against the easy life to which running, among other things, offered an alternative. And the ultimate in running? —THE MARATHON.

As well as the sizes of marathon fields beginning to grow, the number of marathon races multiplied. In October 1976 the author flew to New York to run in the New York City Marathon, the first time the race had started on the Verrazano-Narrows Bridge, and it included the five boroughs of New York—Staten Island, Brooklyn, Queens, the Bronx and Manhattan. This was another spectacular mass-marathon field of more than 2000 runners. Returning in 1977, the author was at the head of a dash of 4823 starters, and yet again in 1978 it was astounding to discover that the 11,400 strong field had virtually fought to take part in the race. The explosion had taken place.

New York was truly the inception of many major cities throughout the world wishing to have a 'people's' marathon of their own. London was not far behind, and with television coverage of the New York Marathon having shown the UK population what was possible, an amazing 21,872 people applied for entry forms for the first London Marathon in 1981. Once more excellent television reporting and media interest served to fuel people's imagination and to demonstrate that it was not just superfit young men who could go the marathon distance, but fat and thin, male and female, mothers and grandmothers, could conquer this event.

Suddenly, the marathon which had provided such drama in all the major athletics games, most especially the Olympics, was within the reach of almost anyone if they so desired. All that was needed finally was the will to go the distance.

All this is a far cry from the old breed of marathon runner. With few exceptions they were athletes who did not have the speed to do well at shorter distances and this fact was reflected in the people who represented their country at the highest level. These competitors too had usually passed their peak at 10,000m or cross-country, and the marathon was the last and longest distance they could move up to, which meant that by and large these runners tended to be older than the average athlete.

Right Frank Shorter (807), winner of the Olympic marathon in 1972, leads from Joss Hermans in the 1977 IAAF World Cup.

For these competitors there was little enjoyment to be gained from actually running the distance, for to push themselves to the limit was painful both physically and mentally. But for a few the rewards of victory made the pain worthwhile, while for others the honour of representing their nation made the hell of the race a thing worth suffering.

The majority of present-day marathon runners, who have no aspirations to win races, have a different approach. The marathon is a social phenomenon and to finish is an achievement in itself.

Below Competitors in the New York Marathon pass through a street in the city.

The London Marathon route crosses Tower Bridge. **Inset** Ideal marathon conditions are damp and cool weather.

Training

As far as training for a marathon is concerned, 'you get out of the training what you put into it'—up to a point.

Let's face it, many people could manage a marathon on no training at all. Therefore one has to define what one wants from this test. Just to finish, no matter what the time, would satisfy a lot of people, but there are more who want to complete the distance in a reasonable time and more still who want to improve their times over their past races. So, having decided what you want out of a marathon, you can then decide what to put into it.

Training log

For maximum productivity of training it is essential that the runner keeps some kind of training log (the author's dates back to 1956) and has a future plan. The purpose of a log is twofold. Firstly, it records accurately what training has occurred historically in producing a given performance, without actually relying on memory which is both fallible and selective. This can then be used with benefit in planning future training. Secondly, it provides the runner with a disciplinary taskmaster—nothing done, nothing to record, and gaps or blank spaces must be left for training runs missed.

*Opposite Marathon competitors often wear plastic dustbin liners before a race and during the early stages to keep warm. **Above** Allison Roe in the start group of the 1981 New York Marathon, as they cross the Verrazano-Narrows bridge.*

Training logs can be as complex or as simple as you like, and the author's is nothing more than a lined exercise book with a page for each week, two lines per training session, with ten lines filled in in red ink for competitions. However, there are printed logs available commercially. Possibly the easiest information to record is the number of miles run, totting these up for a weekly summary, plus an annual summary (if you keep at it that long!). A very few people are content to record the amount of time they have run,

but miles are far more significant and time could be added to the distance information for those who are interested.

It is important to be reasonably accurate with the distances recorded and these can be measured in two simple ways. One is from a map using a piece of thread to trace your course, measuring the length of thread and converting this to miles from the scale of the map. Ordnance Survey maps are particularly useful in this respect and are equally useful in providing new and interesting training routes. The other is using the mileometer of a car, providing the run is along a public highway, although this method should never be used by race organizers in determining the distance of their course!

The time taken for each run can be recorded using a lightweight plastic runner's chronograph. This must be purely for interest's sake, and viewed objectively and not obsessionally. There was a time in the author's career when time began to mean so much that he was practically racing each training run to get a 'good' time, and that was bringing no benefit at all. When a slow time was run he used to get worried and it got so bad that one day he wrote in the log, 'Threw the stop watch away'. The runs were far more enjoyable after that! Now he looks at the times objectively only!

Also body weight can be recorded after each run, where possible. Again this is just for interest's sake and through experience the author has learned what his best racing weight is and has observed that his weight increases when 'resting', or running low mileage, and that his winter weight is greater than that of summer.

In a log, this information can be supplemented by details of the kind of training undertaken in a particular run (more of this later) plus comments on how one felt and what the weather was like. Other people will record their pulse rate at rest or on waking, and one can work out the miles per hour or minutes per mile run in order to observe progress.

A record of daily/weekly mileage is vital and any further observations will depend on the interest of the runner.

Planning

For those people who wish to achieve certain targets or goals, which will probably be related to getting the best out of themselves, it is essential that they plan. The training log may record the progress (or otherwise) of training and provide evidence of beneficial training sessions or methods which have not been constructive, but it is acting only as a history. A plan accommodates the future, and should be on both macro and micro levels.

The macro plan should take in the whole year when marathon races and competitions at other distances will be penned in on the appropriate weekends. The author has always had a home-made year planner with his training log in order to be aware of what he is training for (or resting from) and, in fact, at the time of his most successful racing, each training session was mapped out for the full year, which took a lot of decision-making out of training. But this was only after learning over the years, by trial and error, with information extracted from training logs, what training was most suitable. So the macro plan indicates the major target races and therefore the build-up periods and rest periods associated with those races.

Rotterdam, 1983, with Rodolfo Gomez, Carlos Lopes, Rob ('Deek') de Castella and Alberto Salazar.

The micro plan or plans may well be decided as the year progresses depending on the experience gained in training for an individual marathon, but the detail here relates to a build-up in mileage and training intensity to peak for a marathon race, followed by the detail of recovery in preparation for the next build-up and the next race.

Mileage

What build-up in mileage? What training intensity? What peak?—these questions will be asked especially by someone who does the same run, the same number of times per week, at the same pace, month in month out. The beginner may be forgiven for his ignorance of training methods; however, there are still international marathon runners who do not fully understand the necessities of build-up, peaking and resting, and so many of them get to the 'big one' overtrained or injured.

So let us first talk about mileage alone before discussing the complexities of speedwork.

This section on training commenced by saying 'you get out of the training (for a marathon) what you put into it—up to a point'. This can be rephrased, in the context of mileage, by saying, 'The more miles you run, the better marathon runner you will be—up to a point'. It is deciding what that point is that is the skill.

Many people with restrictions on their time may never be able to find what the upper limit point is, and they must be content with making the most of what time/mileage they have available. But if we take an ideal situation, where adequate time is available to discover this upper limit, the runner must experiment. The results of the experiments will appear in the training log and the correct conclusions can be drawn.

Above the upper limit of mileage the runner will become constantly fatigued, be prone to infections, e.g. sore throats and colds, marathon performance will go down and the runner may well become injured. This upper limit will depend on personal factors, but we are talking of say 140 miles per week for the very top runner, possibly higher in exceptional cases. This does not mean you have to run 140 miles per week to be a top marathoner even if you are a talented runner, it is just a 'ball-park' figure for an upper limit from the author's own experience of marathon runners. The author knows of one marathon runner who has achieved just over 2 hr 10 min. for the marathon on 80 miles per week. If you are over 40 years of age, the upper limit of mileage may well be in the 70–80 miles per week range.

What of the lower limit? Well, the lower limit is zero miles per week. There are people who have 'finished' marathons on no training, but between zero and the upper limit there is a whole spectrum of improvement.

How then to achieve this upper limit of mileage? One run a day? Twice a day? Every day? Again it comes down to personal circumstances, individual preferences and the time available. There are several schools of thought on the lengths of training runs; i.e. is one long run better than two short ones? The author's own view is that ultimately it is the cumulative miles that count. Having a full-time job, and a family, it is far easier to take small blocks of time out of a day than a large chunk, and hence to get his miles in the author has always run twice a day. He *had* to when topping 120/130 miles per week, and it fits in well now, even when 70 miles per week is his optimum.

Some people report great difficulty in running first thing in the morning and there is no doubt that it is harder then than in the afternoon or evening, but one can become accustomed to it, and for anyone who is very busy, and who has pressures on time during the day, it is a run that no-one can take away from you. No-one is arriving unexpectedly or wants to make an appointment at 7.00 a.m.!

Therefore if you look at a morning run, if it is only 3 miles and five times, it is an extra 15 miles per week in total. And the tiredness or lethargy of morning running can be regarded positively if you imagine that you are accustoming your body and mind to function through discomfort, which is what they must inevitably do at the end of a marathon race.

Another way of boosting total mileage, in addition to including a valuable training tool into your repertoire, is a weekly 'long run'. This can vary between 8 miles and usually 20 miles, depending on what a short run is for you, and traditionally, among serious runners, this is done on a Sunday. The advent of Sunday races, not necessarily marathons, has made this somewhat more difficult, but even the semi-serious marathon runner should be contemplating a run of around 18 miles three weeks before a marathon event, if only to gain confidence.

Considering the serious runner, who would regularly run a 20 miler on a weekend, this run bestows considerable, if unexplained, positive training effects on the body. It may be related to a complete turnover of glycogen within the body and with this a burning-off of body fats to produce a long-term reduction in body weight. Whatever it is, the long run appears to work.

To return to the author's experience, when running anything under 2 hr 20 min., 120 miles per week was achieved by running to work and back each day, the minimum distance being the 7 miles to work, plus a race on Saturday and a 20 miler on Sunday. Nowadays, he continues with twice a day, except for once only on Sunday, and is quite content to run just $2\frac{1}{2}$ miles most mornings. On Sundays 13 to 15 miles is far enough, especially as this is run alone. The longer runs are saved for races—marathons!

EXTRAORDINARY MARATHON RACE

1. *The Princess of Wales and her children witnessing the arrival of the competitors at the starting post.* 2. *J. J. Hayes (U.S.A.) winner in 2 hours 55min. 18 2-5sec.* 3. *J. Forshaw (U.S.A.), third.* 4. *A. R. Welton, fourth.* 5. *W. Wood (Canada), sixth.* 6. *P. Dorando (Italy), who arrived first but was disqualified, falls for the second time on entering the Stadium.* 7. *Dorando breaks the tape absolutely sent in 2 hours 55min. 46 2-5sec.* 8. *C. Hefferon (South Africa), going through Ruislip, he was placed second in 2 hours 56min. 6sec.* 9. *Competitors coming down Castle Hill at Windsor.* 10. *General view of the Stadium, waiting the arrival of the competitors.* 11. *R. T. Clark, the first British competitor to finish, being 12th, in 3 hours 16min. 8 2-5sec.*

Today's marathon distance was set in the 1908 Olympic Marathon, also notable for the disqualification of Dorando Pietri who collapsed and was aided before he crossed the line (photo 7); **Above** In the lead. **Right** Eventual winner, John Hayes (USA).

117

Pace

Having decided on an optimum practical mileage, or even having decided to experiment to find out what this optimum maximum mileage is, the question of pace arises. How fast should you run?

There is one theory which says that it is sufficient to run slowly, or 'relaxed', all the time—the long slow distance (LSD) theory. The author does not adhere to this theory as a complete training method, but would say that the majority of running should be at a relaxed pace, a pace at which you could comfortably converse if you were running with a partner or at which you could talk without gasping if someone stopped you to ask for directions!

This relaxed pace should relate to most runs whether you are running once a day, or twice a day, mornings and evenings, mornings and lunchtimes, or lunchtimes and evenings, whatever is convenient. Certainly the long (Sunday) run should be easy; who wants to be pushing it for 15 or 20 miles especially if it is the day after a (Saturday) race?

So what of the runs when the pace is not easy? At the correct time of the year or during the build-up to an important race, two 'work' sessions per week plus a shorter distance (than the marathon) race at the weekend should be introduced into the training routine. If there is no race a third 'work' session should be incorporated on Saturday.

Work sessions

These 'non-easy' runs have been termed 'work' sessions; serious runners would probably call them 'speed-work' or 'speed sessions'. What is their value? Well, they can contribute towards a training effect in three ways.

Firstly, they can decrease boredom of one-pace running, as a variety of 'work' sessions can be used.

Secondly, they increase the work load of training causing the body to adapt, to grow stronger and fitter, and in many cases teach the body to operate anaerobically or 'without oxygen', which state can occur in the marathon if the runner at any stage is operating at the limit of his pace or is having to really pile on the speed at the end of a race to beat a competitor or indeed a time goal. (See also page 32.)

Thirdly, they allow the legs to increase their range of movement, by kinetic stretching, so that at race pace they are not being required to operate with extensions they have never experienced before. (See stretching exercises on pages 23–26.)

Most 'training methods' revolve around particular types of work sessions or speedwork, and guidance as to the various possibilities available is accessible to athletes through personal communications, seminars and specialist magazines and books. It does no harm to digest all of the recommendations in these sources, but it is important to retain a completely open mind

Above *Priscilla Welch and Sarah Rowell of Great Britain.* **Opposite** *Charlie Spedding, winner of the 1984 Mars London Marathon and 1984 Olympic bronze medallist, is also an accomplished 5000m and 10,000m runner.*

before putting any ideas or combination of ideas into practice. Even then it must be a question of trial and error with the personal training log revealing the answer, the formula, in the long term.

Some examples of the type of speed/work sessions that may be found in the literature are listed below:

Fartlek A Scandinavian word meaning 'speed-play'. Essentially this technique involves running with bursts of speed (after a couple of easy miles to warm up) over distances of anything from 50m to 800m, or further, as the runner pleases, followed by an easy running recovery phase until the runner wants to 'go' again. If Fartlek sessions are done over the same course, the bursts of fast running tend to become formalized, that is they come at the same places, and for the same distances, each run—up a certain hill—from one tree to another—between seven or eight lamp-posts, etc. And there is nothing wrong with that. (See also page 36.)

Interval work This can be achieved on the track with, for instance, 20 × 400m with 200m jog recovery; but it does not have to be 20. It could be 10, or three sets of four, with 800m jog between each set; or they could be 200m runs, or 600m or 800m, or further, or pyramid sessions: running 200m, then 400m, 600m and 800m and back down again—the varieties are endless. Alternatively, if a track is not easily accessible, the intervals and recovery could be timed on a watch while running on road or country. (See also pages 32–34.)

Long fast running This would entail a run at racing speed (for the marathon), or even faster, over 4, 5 or 6 miles, or perhaps further if the runner can accommodate this. At one stage in his career, when quite successful, the author found sessions such as this particularly onerous and had to omit them from his repertoire as they were not enjoyable. It was not a question of being soft, but these sessions were so disagreeable that they were almost dreaded. Therefore, they were dropped.

Hill work This consists of running hard up hills, and easily down, in the middle of a longer run, the distance to and from the hill being used as warm-up and warm-down respectively.

When

Having discussed 'work' sessions, when should these be attempted in relation to a week's running? Again, this is 'micro' planning, and taking a 'classic' training/racing week, with a race on a Saturday—not necessarily a marathon, preferably a shorter distance race (but more of that later)—the following is suggested.

Saturday:	Race
Sunday:	Long run, easy
Monday:	Work session
Tuesday:	Easy
Wednesday:	Work session
Thursday:	Easy
Friday:	Easy

This pattern allows the body to recover from, and adapt to, Monday's training load with an easy run on Tuesday, and provides two further days of recovery, easy running or 'rest', following Wednesday's work, before a racing effort on Saturday, which in fact will be the hardest training session of the week! For Sunday races, rearrange the weekly training session accordingly.

Where to run

Many people worry about training on roads because of the hardness of the surface but, in fact, with the cushioning available in modern training shoes, this need not be a worry and, after all, the event you are training for will take place on a road surface. In foreign or unfamiliar places, or at night time, it may well be the only surface available for running, but do remember to be careful of traffic. At all times face the oncoming traffic; as the old hands say, 'at least you know when to jump'. At night, make sure you are visible with light coloured clothing or preferably some reflective overvest, armbands, or other devices or attachments.

The author has never held with the recommendation of training on grass, often given to runners who are injured or recovering from injury. Most of the surfaces available, those edging roads or pavements, or fields, have the unevenness of pastureland and carry the risks of further injury due to twisting unexpectedly on unsure footing. Therefore, unless you have access to a friendly golf course or well tended, well reconnoitred playing field, 'keep off the grass!'

Far more interesting are footpaths and trails through the countryside and on river or canal banks. These surfaces provide a change which is softer underfoot than roads but, most importantly, lead normally to aesthetically pleasing surroundings away from the noise, pollution, and potential danger of vehicular traffic, not to mention people.

Some people like to have hills to run, for variety, but these are not necessary for success and in fact some of the author's most successful fell (hill) race results were achieved when he lived and trained in Fallowfield, Manchester, which is dead flat.

It is debatable whether to plan variety in the training routes you seek out and run, and most people would say that the greater the variety the better. However, there have been times when the author has run to work over the same route for years on end, and has accepted it without qualm, being happy to cover the familiar ground almost automatically, and allow thoughts to occupy the time; a kind of kinetic meditation. But the same route can become boring.

Alone or in company?

More than 95% of the author's 106,000+ recorded miles of running have been completed alone, possibly more through circumstance than choice, but it has worked well. The main advantages of this solitary training have been that the pace, distance and method of training have all been to suit him alone. Additionally, the 'kinetic meditations' have been enjoyed with little distraction.

There is no doubt, however, that company and conversation can make the miles fly by on an easy run, with people of similar ability. Training alone, after about 1½ hours of running, 'free thoughts' start to dry up, and the mind starts to fill with questions such as, 'How far to go?' With partners, conversation can usually be easily sustained for 2½ hours.

Some people need the stimulus of having company, that is meeting someone for training, to get them out and, indeed, in the case of women, in the interest of safety, having someone to run with may well be essential. The disadvantages for the very serious runner of training with someone else are that the pace may not be quite right. The speed may be too fast or too slow; or a compromise may have to be reached over a 'work' session, either over-stretching or under-stressing one of the runners. And, of course, when you are training with another athlete, you cannot step out of work, or out of your front door, or depart from a training venue exactly when you want because someone else is involved, and if they are late, it could lead to a lot of wasted time. But obviously there are compromises, the two extremes being all running alone and all running in company.

Peaking

The author considers that, at the top level, it is only possible to give all-out efforts in a marathon three times a year. Some low-key races could certainly be run, treating them as training runs, but serious efforts should be restricted to three times a year. And the planning must begin counting back three or four months before the marathon of your choice.

There should be a gradual build-up of mileage during this period of time, using approximately one third of the build-up time you have allotted yourself, so that, for instance, one month into a three month build-up, you have reached your optimum maximum mileage. Then is the time to introduce 'work' sessions into the regime. Again these should be gradually built up both in number of repetitions, intervals, length of Fartlek and intensity of effort until, two thirds of the way into the build-up, maximum work load has been achieved and will be maintained until one week before the big race, when 'tapering down' should begin. That is, a gradual diminution in miles per run over the week, until you get down to about two miles of easy running the day before the race.

After a marathon race it is essential to take four weeks' 'active rest'. This means doing nothing but easy running, except for non-serious short distance races, which should be fun, dropping to around 25% of maximum mileage for two weeks, followed by two more weeks at 30% of maximum mileage. You will then be ready to start building up your next peak.

Peaking in association with the 'active rest' is possibly the most important and most neglected aspect of marathon training in the UK. It is impossible to train at maximum mileage for long periods at a time. The body becomes either exhausted or injured, both conditions precipitating a 'rest', an *enforced* rest.

The author knows this from bitter experience, having failed to finish in the European Games Marathon held in Belgrade, Yugoslavia, in September 1962, dropping out at the 30km point.

In conditions of poor visibility it is advisable to wear reflective bands or a reflective bib when running.

The histogram from the author's book *The Long Hard Road Part 1: 'Nearly to the Top'* (overleaf, page 122) clearly illustrates around 90 miles per week for all the year until November when he realized something serious was wrong. In fact the 90 miles per week stretched unbroken back to September 1961, and included 'work' sessions nine times per week including races! This contrasts clearly with a further histogram from *The Long Hard Road Part 2: 'To the Peak and Beyond'* (overleaf, page 123), showing his most successful year, 1970, when he won the famous Boston Marathon, followed by the Commonwealth Games Marathon, Edinburgh, in 2 hr 09 min. 28 sec. The peaks and the 'rests' show up very obviously.

Incidentally the end of that year shows the mileage topping out at 160 miles per week, which caused the marathon time to 'slump' to 2 hr 15 min. in the Fukuoka Marathon, Japan—an experiment that failed and was not repeated!

Often athletes who have gone through an enforced rest, through injury or exhaustion, come back to perform extremely well after this rest. The planned active 'rests' being advocated will enable a runner to produce the best results at the right time, and not after injuries which often seem to arrive when least welcome.

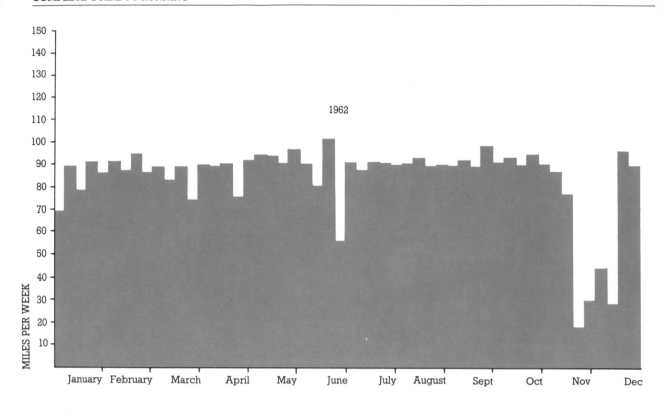

Shorter-distance races

Although many new runners begin the sport with the intention of finishing a marathon, most will go on to include shorter-distance races in their programme, even if the marathon remains the main goal; and this is an excellent thing, as the shorter race efforts will certainly benefit marathon performances.

Looking at the sport at the highest level (and, after all, the strivings of the less talented or less dedicated runners are but a duller mirror image of the star athletes), the best training a marathon runner can adopt is that which a 10,000m runner would apply. Conversely the training for a marathon will equip a runner to reach his or her potential at 10,000m, 10 miles or half-marathon. The best marathon runners around are also exceptional 10,000m and 5000m runners, and some are even capable of breaking 4 minutes for the mile!

As well as the satisfaction of completing a marathon, or doing a good time, there is an excellent social aspect to the sport of running, and with the limit to the number of marathon races which are physically acceptable in a year, this social side to running can be continued with weekly sub-marathon distance competitions. As indicated in the previous section on

Right Joyce Smith, former UK record holder, at 44 the oldest competitor in the 1984 Olympic Marathon.

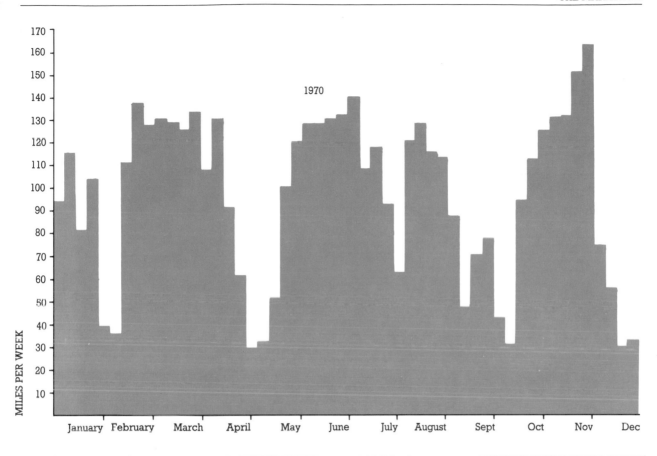

1970

training, the shorter-distance race will be the hardest 'work' session of the week.

But in addition to that, for the more serious athlete, the shorter races are exercises in pace judgement and provide continuous education and experience in tactics. You can take more risks with the pace in these races than in the marathon, perhaps to find out what you are really capable of or, on the other hand, what speed or effort is too much for you!

However, there are other things beside road races you can try out, for example, cross-country running in winter, or fell (hill and mountain) running all the year round, or even track running. Each has its own requirements of skills and strength and, who knows? —there may be a hidden talent.

Opposite Carlos Lopes (465) in 1984 won the World Cross-Country Championship, was the second fastest ever 10,000m runner and won the gold medal in the Olympic Marathon, at the age of 37. **Below** *Geoff Smith, winner of the 1984 Boston Marathon.* **Right** *Winner of the 1983 New York Marathon, Rod Dixon of New Zealand.*

Supplementary training

Are there other aids to training or exercise which would complement, or be a substitute for, running?

Weight training could well be beneficial, using light weights and many repetitions, to tone up the upper body, but body-building as such is probably detrimental to marathon performance.

Swimming is a useful activity for an injured runner in keeping muscles working and exercising the heart and lungs, but by no means should be substituted for running by the fit athlete if there is a choice.

Cycling is a useful supplementary training activity as it can provide extra cardio-vascular training without the pounding and jarring of running on the roads, and it also builds up the quadriceps, the big muscles at the front of the thighs. Actually riding a bike is the most attractive, but obviously circumstances such as weather or traffic sometimes preclude this, in which case it is equally useful to use a stationary exercise cycle.

Skipping could also substitute for running if, for instance, you are snowbound or perhaps at sea. If you get out of breath it is doing you good.

At the end of it all, though, running is best!

WHAT TO TAKE TO A RACE

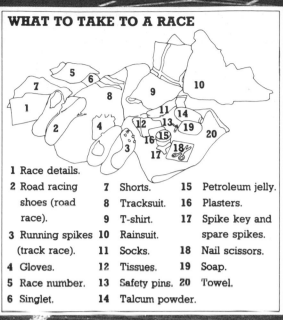

1 Race details.
2 Road racing shoes (road race).
3 Running spikes (track race).
4 Gloves.
5 Race number.
6 Singlet.
7 Shorts.
8 Tracksuit.
9 T-shirt.
10 Rainsuit.
11 Socks.
12 Tissues.
13 Safety pins.
14 Talcum powder.
15 Petroleum jelly.
16 Plasters.
17 Spike key and spare spikes.
18 Nail scissors.
19 Soap.
20 Towel.

Pre-race preparation

Having got to within a week of your chosen marathon race, at the *peak* of fitness, what do you do then? Well, in that last seven days you taper down. That is, you progressively reduce the mileage run each day so that at the end of those seven days the total miles will be roughly half of what your peak training has been. For instance, if you have been running 70 miles a week, you would want to come down to, say, 35 miles. If the race were on a Sunday, those miles might well be accommodated as follows: Sunday 10; Monday 7; Tuesday 5; Wednesday 5; Thursday 4; Friday 2; Saturday 2. Yes, it is useful to go out the day before a marathon and run a little. It serves to loosen the muscles and joints and soothes the pre-race nerves, the run acting as a sort of mental rehearsal.

Sooner or later you are bound to come across the 'glycogen loading diet', which the author pioneered in marathon running back in 1969 and with which he has had a great deal of experience.

The theory is that for a certain number of days, three being the best, you deprive the body of carbohydrate. This depletes the amount of glycogen in the muscle tissues. After these three days you eat lots of carbohydrate and the muscles grab this to form glycogen. But, instead of returning to normal levels of glycogen, the muscles over-compensate and take on an extra load which is available as extra fuel to the marathon runner. The notorious 'wall' occurs in the marathon when the easily convertible fuel, glycogen, runs out, usually at around 18 or 20 miles. Therefore, using the diet, the 'wall' is hit much later.

Some people advocate the carbohydrate loading regime only, missing out the starvation part, and this makes a little sense as one could argue that, with heavy training, the muscles are continually in a state of relative glycogen depletion, and therefore a combination of low mileage and high carbohydrate diet produces a 'glycogen loading' effect anyway.

Before detailing the author's version of 'the diet', the warning should be given that, by completely avoiding carbohydrates in food intake, the athlete is running into danger, and a negative effect could well occur. Assuming a Sunday marathon, Monday, Tuesday, Wednesday should be low-carbohydrate days. Some people have advocated a 'long run to exhaustion' on the Sunday or Monday, reducing carbohydrate thereafter, but there is nothing more ridiculous than to push oneself to exhaustion the week before a marathon. To return to the author's version, Monday and Tuesday would be 'work' training sessions, and these would suffice to deplete glycogen reserves. Low carbohydrate would mean omitting sugar, chocolate, sweets, potatoes, pasta, bread, pastries, etc.

Left Steve Jones, new holder of the world marathon best with 2 hr. 8 min. 5 sec. (Chicago, 1984) is also a world-class track and cross-country runner.

However, one banana, one apple, one orange and four crisp biscuits or thin slices of toast are suggested. Complete omission of carbohydrate may lead to hallucinations, depression, burning of fats, which will be needed on marathon day, and possibly, in extreme cases, the burning of protein, i.e. the very muscles you are going to use for propulsion.

On day 4, Thursday, the temptation will be to load up on carbohydrates to satisfy the craving that will have developed, and one should succumb to that temptation for it is a major pleasure to be savoured! But, after that, Friday and Saturday should be back to a more or less normal diet as runners usually eat lots of carbohydrate anyway. Attempting to force down more extra carbohydrate could lead to stomach upsets.

But what can you eat on low-carbohydrate days? Meat, fish, cheese, green vegetables, eggs, peas, beans and carrots. Together with the low amounts of carbohydrate previously mentioned, that should keep you going.

On race day, a staple pre-race meal can be two slices of bread and butter with jam and a cup of tea, three hours before the race. For the marathon the time lag can be reduced to two hours, especially if it is an early morning start. For an afternoon start, you could well have a breakfast of cereal, toast and jam. Egg, bacon and sausage-type repasts will serve no useful purpose, and could possibly harm performance.

While on the subject of diet, we should consider liquid intake before the race, especially if the weather is likely to be hot. If it looks like being a scorching day take plenty of liquid before the start, perhaps as much as two pints. Just plain water is fine, but something lightly flavoured, to be palatable, is all right too. Take the last cupful just before the start but remember also to go to the toilet *before* the gun goes, otherwise you may have to lose valuable time on a pit-stop.

At all levels, the couple of hours leading up to the start of a race can lead to considerable strain, so remember to pack your bag the night before and have a check list, starting with what you will need before the race and finishing with what you require after the race. For example: racing singlet and shorts, number or registration certificate, extra safety pins, T-shirt or long sleeve shirt in case it is cold, tracksuit or wet-weather suit, shoes—well broken in (no new shoes), socks, towel, sticking plasters, post-race drinks, food.

When you get close to the start, if it is wet and cold make sure you have someone there to take your tracksuit before the gun, or alternatively wear a plastic dustbin liner you can discard. There is little to be gained from 'warming-up'; perhaps jog for 300m or 400m, but plenty of stretching would suffice.

If it is a hot day, keep off your feet and in the shade

At the start of many marathons marker boards indicate where you should position yourself.

as much as possible before the race. Do not warm up and do not wear a tracksuit—*keep cool*. Wet your hair and your limbs with water to assist cooling.

Finally, on the start line go to your allocated section. You will know from experience, or by an intelligent guess, what final time you are capable of, so go to that section of the start indicated for you. If you do not, and try to get to the front, you will hinder the faster runners and will run the risk of causing an accident or being pushed over, which is the last thing you want.

The start

In today's megafield marathons, the runner standing in the correct segment of the field will not have much choice over the pace for the first two or three miles, because of the crowding, and this is a good thing as, in view of the excitement that has been building up before the race, if the runner were presented with an open road, adrenalin would be running so high that it is almost certain he or she would fly off, only to collapse in a heap a few miles down the road.

A novice marathon runner should try to run the race at an even pace. You will have a good idea of what time you can do from previous marathons or from long training runs. Try to stick to that pace and do not get carried away in the thrill of the day. Almost all marathons these days have each individual mile marked; work out the time you expect for each mile, and stick to it. Slow down if you have gone over your pace!

For the more experienced marathon runner the first half of the race should be slightly faster than the second—not deliberately so, but equal output of effort will produce a slower pace as the going gets tougher at the end.

For top-class marathon runners the pace at the start will depend mostly on tactics, but the very best runners have an inbuilt sense which regulates their maximum pace and prevents them going over the top and into 'oxygen debt' when surely they would 'blow up' and have to slow down, recover, and then get going again.

The race

In a race such as the London Marathon the top 20 or so runners will be actually competing and racing throughout the race. The rest of the runners, excepting the minor battles that go on throughout the field, will be aiming for a reasonable time or, indeed, just to finish. The latter will not care about times, only about how their bodies feel, and concentration on keeping moving is all they need.

Beginners or progressing marathon runners will be sticking to 'splits', that is watching the time it takes to cover one mile or five miles in order to monitor their progress. This is sensible, but for novice marathon runners it is more than sensible—it is essential. The advice for these runners is to err on the side of caution. If you want to put some effort into the race, wait until the last couple of miles; rather that than an overfast first couple of miles, followed by a tortuous struggle for another 24 miles. If you finish full of beans, up the pace in your next marathon until you find your true capability.

For the top marathon runners, the race can be a fascinating tactical battle, and different tactics have developed over the last couple of decades. In the author's heyday, 1962–76, it was literally 'survival of the fittest'. In the 1960s, he felt that he had to be able to run for 15 miles at 5 minute mile pace (2 hr 11 min. pace) and 'let time flow over his head'. Then the race began, and runners dropped off the leading pack, one by one, until the last one at the front won the race. In his two most notable victories (Boston 1970 and Edinburgh 1970) the pace was much faster than 5 minute miling, and in the latter race, the Commonwealth Championship, there were only three people left at six miles —the author, Jerome Drayton (Canada) and Philip Ndoo (Kenya). At ten miles (47 min. 48 sec.) Drayton had just dropped away and by the turn (1 hr 02 min. 35 sec.) the author was away on his own.

Now, with a greater number of people capable of around 2 hr 10 min., we are seeing races where a large group stays together until near the end of the race, when the pack is decimated by 'surges', or dramatic increases in pace, eventually leaving a winner. Or the pace might gradually be wound up at the *end* of a race, getting faster and faster, again until the winner breaks away on his own. These tactics have produced several top-class races where the second

Right *Rotterdam 1983, won by Rob de Castella from Carlos Lopes.* **Below** *Massed start of the London Marathon.* **Opposite** *It will take a fast, relaxed uninhibited pace by someone such as Juma Ikangaa of Tanzania to take the marathon record below 2 hr 8 min.*

Feeding station in the New York Marathon, with the litter of earlier competitors.

Waldemar Cierpinski (GDR) 1976 and 1980 Olympic marathon champion, demonstrates the folding of a paper cup for drinking on the run.

half of the marathon has been faster than the first.

However, the marathon record has stuck at 2 hr 8 min. for almost 15 years now, and these last tactical races have only approached the record, despite the advent of pace-makers. The record *will* go below 2 hr 8 min., but it will take the old tactic—fast, relaxed and uninhibited from the start, as practised by someone like Juma Ikangaa of Tanzania—to take it down.

Naturally, it will need ideal conditions to improve on the record—cool weather, little wind, possibly a light drizzle and a flat course. A hot day normally precludes fast times, and extra precautions have to be taken. Ideally a mesh singlet should be worn which allows air to pass over sweat, or water-moistened skin, and to create a cooling effect by evaporation. This evaporation occurs less in humid atmospheres, hence the greater degree of discomfort that is felt on muggy days. Women should wear singlets with the lower part in mesh. Shorts should be brief and free from chafing. The whole outfit should be white where possible, when running in direct sunlight, as darker colours, especially black and navy, absorb the heat of the sun's rays, thus adding extra unwanted heat to the body.

As described above, the body perspires when it gets hot to create a film of moisture, which cools the body by evaporation in the stream of air that passes over it during movement. Copious perspiring on hot days can lead to the risk of dehydration and, therefore, as well as being topped up with liquid before the race, it is essential to take fluids during the race itself, water being the most preferable.

You should start to drink before you feel the need. If you wait until your body is crying out for liquid, you are too late, as it takes some time for the fluid to dissipate around the body, by which time you may be a stretcher case.

Drinking on the run is difficult and can lead to discomfort if you get sticky drinks all over your face and fingers. If you can arrange to have your own fluids handed to you in plastic bottles with narrow necks, so much the better; the majority will have to make do with what is on the drinks table. Plastic cups are impossible to drink from while running. A mouthful is all you can hope to take before the liquid has splashed away. Paper cups are much better as you can fold the tops to virtually seal them, then drink out of the corner—try this with a plastic cup and it breaks up. The technique is to pour or squeeze the liquid into the bottom of your mouth, keep your mouth open, breathe a couple of times to get your breath back then swallow. And so on. If you are in desperate trouble: *stop* for four or five seconds, drink the lot down and then proceed. Those few seconds lost there could mean minutes gained over the latter stages.

So much for the inside. Do not neglect the outside of the body on hot days, and make full use of any sponges. Pick a full sponge, squeeze some on to the top of your head, the back of your neck, wipe your face with it, then your arms, and finally, with the sponge now just more or less damp, wipe your thighs—big muscles with plenty of surface area to assist cooling. This method of sponging minimizes the amount of water which may get into your shoes, making them heavy. Heavy shoes means more work to do lifting them, and wet shoes present the possibility of unstable gait with your feet sliding about inside them.

Observing all the foregoing advice, you should reach the finish and, with a little bit of luck, in the time you were hoping for.

The finish

And after the finish, what then? Well, whatever your standard, if you have observed the advice on macro-planning and resting you know you have an easy four weeks ahead, and that knowledge alone should have given an extra boost to your performance.

At the immediate finish, if you have won the race you will not have a lot of deciding to do; the media will probably take up your time before the award ceremony, and anyway you will feel on top of the world. Second or third place produces a totally different emotion, especially after a close battle, but, as for all the rest down the field, try to keep moving. If it is cold, get to some warm clothing immediately. Your resistance is down, your body is beaten, and you need to get wrapped up; find a hot drink.

If it has been a hot day, again, keep moving for a while, walking, and drink as much as you can. Remember you have really beaten up your body and you need to provide it with the things with which to repair itself, starting straight away. If some of your immediate pain is due to blisters you should seek attention from any post-race medical facility. If there

A runner in the European Marathon picks up a drink at full speed.

are no medical facilities, you may decide to 'pop' any surface blisters as described earlier. Deep-down blisters, under the ball of the foot or heel, may need surgical treatment, otherwise you will have to be patient and let them dissipate naturally.

For the relief of immediate post-race stiffness in the joints and painful aching muscles (often referred to by runners as 'stiffness' also), a hot bath works wonders. Everyone is sore in the hours and days after a race and that can be straightened out with time. To assist this you must make a conscious effort to eat well, with proteins, meats, fish and eggs sent down to the stomach to provide the building blocks to repair muscle tissues.

With this in mind, physically the best thing you could do after a marathon would be to drink lots of water or electrolyte drink, have a good meal, and go to bed early. Again, physically, the last thing doctors would advise you to do is drink lots of beer as this could lead to further dehydration. However, there is a *psychological* need too, after the race. The release from the weeks and months of training and the triumph of finishing the marathon virtually demands a celebration, a wake, a letting down of the hair. If you are not happy with your performance, you can always drown your sorrows!

In the days after the race everyone has sore muscles, perhaps to the extent of having to manhandle oneself down stairs. But you can stretch a bit, go out, and very gingerly break into a jog for a couple of miles. The next day you go a bit further and so on until after six or seven days you are running freely again. This does not mean that you have recovered, or you will have recovered, in a week. It can take a month to get over a hard marathon physically, and around

Opposite top Officials will guide marathon competitors down funnels at the finish. Opposite bottom At the end of a race it is important to keep warm; here competitors are wearing foil space blankets. Below Joan Benoit, the women's marathon gold medallist at the 1984 Olympics.

three months to get over it mentally, if you have really flogged yourself.

Aim to be racing again over short distances two weeks later (one week later if you cannot resist!) but if you want to run well, remember the four weeks' active rest and an eight to twelve week build-up to the next marathon.

Superstars

For those with the ability, the advice in the foregoing is sufficient to get you to the top, given drive and ambition. There is one extra tip for those in this category: *never drop out.* Top marathoning is not for quitters. If that option is in your repertoire, you will use it: *quitting should not be an option.*

Alberto Salazar (USA). Former world record holder with 2 hr 08 min. 13 sec. set in New York in 1981, and also the Boston Marathon record holder. A world class 5000m and 10,000m track runner, he has a superb collection of top marathon times to his credit. These crucifying runs may have taken their toll and his last four performances have been defeats.

Rob de Castella (Australia). Not everyone's picture of a marathon runner, he burst into the scene in 1981 with a 2 hr 08 min. 18 sec. victory in Fukuoka, just outside Salazar's world record. Since then his devastating late surges have brought him the Commonwealth Championship, 1982, with 2 hr 09 min. 18 sec., the unofficial World Championship, Rotterdam, 1983, with 2 hr 08 min. 37 sec., and the official World Championship, Helsinki 1983 with 2 hr 10 min. 03 sec. He finished 5th in the 1984 Olympic marathon.

Derek Clayton (Australia). Although his time of 2 hr 08 min. 34 sec. in Antwerp, 1969, is doubted in some circles, he certainly had the ability, having won Fukuoka in 1967 with a world record of 2 hr 09 min. 37 sec. A legend in the late 1960s (200 training miles per week) he was thought to be invincible for a while, yet when it came to the major Games, like his compatriot Ron Clarke, he was unable to come up with the goods.

Bill Rodgers (USA). Virtually unknown until he won the Boston Marathon in 1975, with 2 hr 09 min. 55 sec. Including that performance, he has won the Boston four times and the New York City Marathon four times. His best time is 2 hr 09 min. 27 sec., Boston, 1979.

Abebe Bikila (Ethiopia). This high-altitude native astounded the world by winning the Rome Olympic Marathon, in 1960, in bare feet. He repeated this victory in the Tokyo Olympics, 1964, this time shod, with an Olympic record of 2 hr 12 min. 11 sec., only five weeks after an appendix operation. Tragically he was paralysed from the waist down in a car accident in 1967 and sadly died in 1973.

Waldemar Cierpinski (East Germany). Not one of the favourites when he ran away from the then current Olympic Champion, Frank Shorter, in the later stages of the 1976 Olympic Marathon, to win in 2 hr 09 min. 55 sec. He virtually disappeared until four years later, when he surfaced to retain his Olympic title in Moscow with 2 hr 11 min. 03 sec. He was third in the World Championships, Helsinki, 1983, with 2 hr 10 min. 37 sec. He did not compete in the 1984 Olympic Marathon because of the Communist boycott.

Grete Waitz in the Gillette London Marathon.

Bill Rodgers, winner of the Boston and New York Marathons four times each.

Joan Benoit on the victory rostrum at the Los Angeles Olympics with Grete Waitz and Ros Mota.

Carlos Lopes (Portugal). Set the Olympic record at Los Angeles aged 37 with a time of 2 hr 9 min. 21 sec. Sprang to prominence finishing second to Rob de Castella in the 1983 Rotterdam Marathon with 2 hr 08 min. 38 sec.

Frank Shorter (USA). Revivalist of the USA's marathon fortunes with his victory in the 1972 Olympics, Munich, his birthplace. His time there was 2 hr 12 min. 19.8 sec. He won the Fukuoka Marathon four times, was second in the Montreal Olympics, and has a personal best time of 2 hr 10 min. 30 sec.

Grete Waitz (Norway). The 'first lady' of world marathon running. She has held the world record four times, the last time for less than 24 hours, when her 2 hr 25 min. 29 sec. in London, 1983, equalling the time of New Zealand's Allison Roe, was broken by Joan Benoit's 2 hr 22 min. 43 sec. in Boston. She has won the New York Marathon five times, and is current World Champion with her 2 hr 28 min. 09 sec. in Helsinki,

1983. An excellent track runner and World Cross-Country Champion several times, she came second to Joan Benoit in the 1984 Olympic Marathon for women.

Steve Jones (Great Britain). In the only marathon he has ever finished, he set the world record of 2 hr 08 min. 05 sec. in the Chicago Marathon, October 1984, leaving both Lopes and de Castella more than one minute behind.

Joan Benoit (USA). Broke the world record at Boston with 2 hr 22 min. 43 sec., a run which included some startling splits: 10 miles, 51 min. 38 sec.; half-marathon, 1 hr 11 min. 20 sec. This is a controversial record as it may be deemed to have been paced (by the men in the race), but nevertheless it is a superb run. She did not compete in the World Championships 1983 as the Boston race was not the official USA trial, but won the first women's Olympic Marathon at Los Angeles in 1984 in 2 hr 24 min. 52 sec.

Kennington Brixton
Streatham Norbury
London Rd Croydon
109
SOUTH CROYDON GARAGE

GHV 116 N

Ultra-distance running

Introduction

'I don't warm up for about ten hours!' So said a straight-faced Mike Newton when once asked why he ran so far. Mike may have an exceptionally slow fuse, but there are thousands of other distance runners who now find the marathon no longer turns them on. For this steadily growing breed, the finish line can be an anti-climax and often one hears the comment: 'I couldn't have gone any faster but I could go around again.'

To a track star or armchair athlete, this may seem outrageous—either the runner is not trying hard enough or he is simply showing off. Indeed, in some cases both are true but most of these athletes are merely acknowledging that their stamina is greater than their speed. For more and more people it would appear that 26.2 miles are just not enough.

So far the stars of the standard marathon have largely resisted the temptation to run at the more comfortable ultra pace, but, even without this influx, the world beyond the marathon is already dividing into two distinct sections: the old-fashioned ultras of up to 24 hours and the new multi-day 'mega-marathons' of up to six days. Journey runs are also coming into vogue but new fixtures are appearing all the time and most of the organizers are able to cope.

Nowadays there are races from 30 to 1000 miles and some of these will be looked at in detail later, along with some of the personalities who run them. There is also guidance as to how you can join them —and perhaps even beat them—in the training section. But before we examine the current scene we ought to look back in time, and even the more sceptical among us will realize that the desire to run far has always been with us, and in certain civilizations, a most natural thing to do. Indeed, long before carbohydrate-loading and air-cushioned soles, our ancestors covered vast distances faster than we do today.

When George Littlewood set the (until 1984) all-time record for six-day racing in 1888, he was actually slowing down! The promoters had asked him to hold back because they feared if he put the distance out of reach, the sport would die through lack of interest. They were right.

That 623¾ mile total stood until July 1984, when Yiannis Kouros ran 635 miles 1023 yd in six days; despite the modern revival, only one runner had previously come within 50 miles of it. This record was the longest surviving of any distance, and is one of the most notable landmarks in the history of athletics—an excellent starting point then for our look into the past.

Littlewood's run was both the jewel in the crown of six-day racing and a nail in its coffin. None of his contemporaries could aspire to such mileage and this Madison Square Garden event signalled the beginning of the end of pedestrianism's golden age. But what an era it had been: both glorious and grotesque as men drove themselves to the limits of human endurance. Fabulous fortunes were won, gambling and cheating flourished in an age of skulduggery and crowd support bordered on hysteria.

Right *Mike Newton, the first runner of modern times to break 500 miles in six days.* **Opposite** *Colin Dixon, Christine Barrett, Mike Newton and Don Choi (left to right) celebrate their achievements at the Trentham Gardens Six Day Race, 1984.*

Almost as remarkable as the survival of the record is our ignorance of this colourful period. In the 1880s, six-day racing was the most popular sport on both sides of the Atlantic and crowds of up to 10,000 a day would cram smoke-filled arenas to see the athletes circling the tiny, eight-laps-to-a-mile track. They would run and they would walk, they would shuffle and they would stagger, they would eat, drink and sleep their way to distances that have so far proved to be beyond the modern runner.

Clad in such apparel as black velvet knee breeches, lavender tights and white ruffled shirts, the competitors would consume delights such as beef and eel broth, egg and sherry concoctions, milk punch and champagne. The more serious among them would take strychnine and belladonna, be treated to scarificators and electric shocks, and all this between mustard baths and occasional attacks from a rival's 'heavies'!

Besides Littlewood, the heroes of the age were men like Charlie Rowell, once a lowly boat boy from Maidenhead who won $20,000 from two races in 1879; Irish Americans Daniel O'Leary and Patrick Fitzgerald; and the Grand Old Man of the sport, Edward Payson Weston.

It was Weston, whose name is given to the modern event in New Jersey, who started it all by becoming the first man to walk 500 miles in six days in 1875. He did it on the 331 ft track of the Washington Street Rink in Newark, New Jersey, and with just 25 minutes to spare. It was the start of a new era for until then Weston had made his name walking back and forth across America and several similar transcontinental journeys stand out from the turnpike era of the century before.

The year 1754 saw the first centurion and four years later George Guest covered 1000 miles in 28 days. 'Go-as-you please' was the theme and pedestrianism the name of the game. Other famous pedestrians in Britain were Foster Powell, who 'walked' regularly between London and York, and Captain Barclay and Abraham Wood who fought the first duel over 24 hours in 1807.

One of the most incredible performances of this or any era is that of Ernest Memsen, a Norwegian who is reported to have run from Paris to Moscow, a distance of 1550 miles in 14 days, 5 hours and 50 minutes. We must assume he ran but he could have been an early tri-athlete as he swam 13 rivers as well!

In the age of the horse and carriage it became commonplace for footmen to be sent ahead of their masters to deliver messages and reserve rooms and

Left Christine Barrett, the latest female 'ultra' star competing in the 1984 Trentham Gardens Six-Day Race, where she broke nine world records: 72 hours, 96 hours, 300 km, 400 km, 300 miles, 500 km, 600 km, 400 miles and six days. **Opposite** Yiannis Kouros, who in July 1984 broke George Littlewood's long-standing six-day best by running 635 miles.

roadside inns. Soon there were rivalries which quickly developed into sport. Races of all distances were organized and occasionally one of the 'masters' would take part as Sir Robert Carey did, walking to Berwick from London in 1589 for a bet.

But, noble though these efforts were, they paled in comparison with those of the peichs of the Turkish Empire who carried the Sultan's mail between Cairo and Constantinople; the Incas, who brought fresh fish hundreds of miles from the sea; and the Irishmen the Vikings used to 'discover' America after their early landings.

But, of course, we have to go back much further than that for the earliest races, and it was the Romans who organized the first track ultra. Using the chariot racing course in the Circus Maximus (about 800 yards), long-distance events were staged and there is a record of one runner having covered some 147 miles.

The most celebrated ultra performance of ancient times is undoubtedly the legendary run by Pheidippides from Athens to Sparta (see pages 104–105). Until recently this hemerodromoi, or messenger, was credited with having started the marathon boom

(albeit in 490 BC) for it was believed he merely ran from the village of Marathon to Athens (some 24 miles). It is generally accepted now that if he ran at all, he would have done the longer distance (some 154 miles) and there is even a race to commemorate that occasion—the Spartathlon, which Yiannis Kouros won in 1983.

So ultra running, and indeed ultra racing, have been with us a long time and practised in a wide variety of arenas. Many countries have their claimants and the outstanding message delivered through the centuries is that it is not such a fantastic performance to run beyond the marathon. That our forefathers generally handled the multi-day runs better than we do is testimony both to their toughness and to our scepticism. It is indeed amazing that with all the aids a runner has today, it took so long to beat George Littlewood. For the best part of a century we were not interested and only now are we beginning to believe such things can be done. When we acquire the knack to go with the belief, we will excel at the long distances and only then will we be complete athletes—masters of speed *and* endurance.

Classics

These days the ultramarathoner not only has the widest choice of events he has ever known but the widest variety of locations. The current fixture list covers races from 30 miles to six days, from the track to the transcontinental, and such places as Westminster Bridge, El Dorado Canyon, the forests of Finland and the Drakensburg Mountains will all echo with the pitter patter of toiling feet.

New races are being joined by resurrected ones and both George Littlewood and Ernest Memsen would be at home on the circuit today, while even Pheidippides would be able to choose where he delivered his message. The Corinthian spirit prevails and while the ultra runner may miss the short, sharp thrill of speed, his experiences can be no less exhilarating.

The Comrades Marathon is not only the oldest of the ultra classics but, arguably, the biggest and the best. Run alternately 'up' and 'down' the sun-soaked highway between Durban and Pietermaritzburg, it now attracts some 5000 runners to its tortuous 56-mile course. The event is part of South African folklore and the Republic takes a holiday to watch, yet it had the humblest of beginnings.

Opposite Winner of the first ever Spartathlon in 1983, Yiannis Kouros holds aloft the Spartathlon Cup. **Above right** Cavin Woodward (15), former world record holder for 100 miles, competes in a 100 km track race at Crystal Palace in 1978. **Right** Don Ritchie breaks the 100 km world record in the same race.

The founder was Vic Clapham of the 'Comrades of the Great War Association', who persuaded 34 entrants to line up in Pietermaritzburg on Empire Day in 1921—and run to the sea. First down the dusty road was one W. Rowan, whose 8 hr 59 min. is, by a long way, the slowest winning time. The following year the legendary Arthur Newton won, but it is more for the performance of Bill Payne that the 1922 race will be remembered.

After stopping for both breakfast and lunch, Bill worked up quite a thirst and proceeded to quench it in true rugby style—he knocked back no less than 12 pints! Later he devoured a dish of curry and rice, poured a bottle of peach brandy after that and still found time for tea and cakes with his family. He eventually finished in over 11 hours—wearing rugby boots!

This is the stuff of which Comrades legends are made but, alas, not enough to win one of the bronze medals that are awarded to all finishers inside 11 hours. The first ten runners home win gold, with the silvers going to all who break seven and a half hours, but it is often the eleventh hour that sees the greatest drama. Runners sprint, stagger, collapse and crawl to the line to beat the pistol crack in a frenzy of excitement that can surpass even the sight of the winner coming in half a day earlier.

The most dramatic up-front finish came in 1967 when local boy, Manie Kuhn, pipped Scotland's Tommy Malone by just one second! Past 'greats' who have won this race at least a hat-trick of times are Arthur Newton, Wally Hayward, Jackie Mekler and Dave Bagshaw, and they have been joined recently by Alan Robb and Bruce Fordyce, the latter now being regarded as perhaps the greatest ultra runner of all time.

Opposite The 54-mile London to Brighton race starts in Westminster at the stroke of 7 am. **Below** Blond South African Bruce Fordyce, perhaps the greatest ultra-distance runner of all time.

One of the old traditions still maintained is to fire a cannon at noon to warn the waiting dignitaries of the winner's impending arrival. Nowadays, the winner will have had his shower and be downing his second beer by the time the noise booms around the valley of the Thousand Hills. Yes, whether it's 'up' or 'down', the course is a killer and names like Mpusheni, Cato Ridge, Umzinduzi and Botha's Hill recall battles of a bloody past. But now English, Zulu and Afrikaaner run shoulder to shoulder united in their conquest of the course.

The current record is 5 hr 30 min. 12 sec. set by Fordyce in 1983—light years ahead of Mr Rowan. Tremendous progress has certainly been made in South African athletics—both in training and integration—but it will have to occur in other aspects of life before this country is allowed back into the international athletics fold, and before the rest of the world can enjoy an event that Britain's Ron Bentley has described as 'the highlight of my life'.

We cannot leave South Africa without mentioning the *Two Oceans* race. Over 56km and held at Easter, it is the ideal warm-up for the Comrades. First staged in 1970 with 26 starters, it has had an even more meteoric rise with thousands now enjoying the beautiful route between the Atlantic and Indian Oceans.

Often compared with the Comrades and believed by many to be the older race, is the 'London to Brighton'. Certainly, the distance (now 53½ miles) is much the same but there the similarity ends. Where the Comrades has charisma the 'Brighton' has charm, and where the Comrades has mass hysteria, the Brighton has only a mild curiosity.

The field has never topped 200 and neither has the number of spectators. Starting on the stroke of seven at the foot of Big Ben, the motley collection of hardy souls sets out for the sea. One or two strollers may look up from their Sunday papers, but the vast majority ignore the runners just as the media tend to do—a great pity as it is one of the most meticulously organized races on the calendar with many of the 'greats' of the ultra world having taken part since 1951.

It is the Blue Riband event for the Road Runners Club, whose founder, Ernest Neville, established the race for whom Arthur Newton had been the inspiration. His solo runs in the 1920s really blazed the trail down the busy A23 but the old professionals had raced to Brighton as long ago as 1837 when John Townsend took 8 hr 37 min.

First winner of the modern race was Lewis Piper of Blackheath, who led home the 32 finishers in 6 hr 18 min. 40 sec., the only occasion the winning time was

Right Ian Thompson, holder of the London to Brighton record.
Opposite En route to Brighton in South London.

over six hours. Bernard Gomersall holds the record for most wins (four in succession) while other notables to reach the Sussex coast first include Don Ritchie, Tom O'Reilly, Tom Richards, John Tarrant and Cavin Woodward with, perhaps most famous of all, Ian Thompson who set the record of 5 hr 15 min. 15 sec. in 1980, and Bruce Fordyce who has won on the last three occasions.

It is indeed ironic that this very British 'tea and toast' event has always appealed more to overseas athletes than to Britons. It is to be hoped that the attitude changes as, in the wake of the ultra boom, the 'Brighton' could become not just a classic but a great occasion.

Other established British ultras include the Isle of Man 40, the Woodford to Southend (40), the Two Bridges (36), the South London Harriers 30, the RRC annual track race (of varying distances) and, also on the track, the Charles Rowell Six-Day race in Nottingham. Recent bi-annual 100 milers are the Ewhurst '100' and the Gloucester '100'.

The 'shorter' ones provide ideal stepping stones to the multi-day megamarathons, but all are real runners' races with small fields and very few spectators. For further information on British ultras the Road Runners Club is the best source. Membership is only £2 a year and for that a runner receives insurance as well as a newsletter.

Whereas South Africa has thousands competing in just a handful of ultra races, the USA stages more events than the rest of the world put together, yet not one of them has what could be called mass participation. But though thinly spread, over-distance enthusiasm is great and among the colourful fixtures on the calendar, a handful stand out.

None more so than the Western States 100 Miler. Frequently described as the 'toughest foot-race in the world', it requires its athletes to run, walk or crawl through 30 miles of deep snow, cross rivers and run, walk or crawl in and out of steaming canyons, enduring temperatures that fluctuate from freezing to over 100°F.

The race skirts the slopes of the Sierra Nevada mountain range and follows a tortuous stretch of a trail along which early settlers found their way to the Californian coast. There is a total altitude gain of 17,040 ft with a loss of 21,970 ft so it is no wonder the long johns are often swapped for the suntan cream.

It all started in 1977 with 17 runners and has grown to 350 which is the maximum the course can cope with out of the 1200 applicants. The start is in Squaw Valley and the finish in Auburn, at the heart of California's gold country. You are given 30 hours in which to complete the course and silver belt buckles are awarded to all those who make it inside 24 hours. Despite the distance, it can still produce an exciting climax, and the 1983 version was the closest yet with

Jim Howard outsprinting Jim King to win by just 31 seconds. His time, 16 hr 7 min. 55 sec., is impressive but, more than most races, this one is about 'taking part'.

Even tougher(!), according to *Ultrarunning Magazine*, is the Old Dominion Cross Country Endurance Run. Not as old or as famous as the Western States Run, it is thought by many aficionados to be more difficult and the field is limited to 75 'serious ultra runners who have completed a 50-mile race in less than nine hours'. The race is a rugged adventure in the Blue Ridge Mountains and Shenandoah River Valley of Virginia. Once again the scenery is spectacular and the mountain ascents a real challenge.

The resurrection of six-day racing occurred at Woodside in California in 1980 and of the twelve modern races no less than seven have been held in the USA. The oldest is the Weston in Pennsauken, New Jersey, and others are the New Astley Belt Race in San Diego and the New York Road Runners Club (NYRRC) race in New York.

Among the many wonderful and weird names are the 'Recover From The Holidays Fat Ass Fifty', while up in Spotted Bear, Montana, another 50 miler rejoices in the title 'Le Grizz'. There's even one called the 'No Bullshit 50'. But the best description must go to the Four Peaks Fifty. Hardly designed for the fainthearted jogger, the advertisement tempts you like this: 'Fifty miles of extreme heat, wind, snow and dust on an out-and-back primitive mountain road and trail. Adequate mental and physical preparation are of utmost importance to each runner, for the Four Peaks are relentless in their challenge. Rattlesnakes and bears inhabit the territory and there is a climb to over 7000 ft elevation and back to the desert floor'.

Australia has only recently appeared on the ultra scene but when it did so, it arrived with a bang. The Sydney to Melbourne 537 Miler had a dream start in 1983 when a 61 year old farmer, Cliff Young, won the race and the hearts of his countrymen with a magnificent performance taking less than six days. Now to be run alternately 'up' and 'down' between Australia's two major cities, it has taken its rightful place as one of the big races on the circuit.

On the continent of Europe there is a plethora of 100km events, but none can be considered classics sufficient to attract runners from across the globe. They are more like 'people's ultras' with some competitors taking up to 24 hours to complete the course —stopping for lunch, dinner and sometimes even a night's rest at a nearby auberge. However, the French have recently introduced two major megamarathons for the very, very serious runner and these are the Six-

Opposite *A competitor in the London to Brighton race arrives at the finish.*

Jours indoors at La Rochelle and the Bordeaux to Paris, run in the time-honoured fashion alternately 'up' and 'down'.

Conditions could not be more diverse: 'La Rochelle' hosts its athletes in the cool confines of a sports drome in October, whereas the road runners are subject to the searing heat and traffic of the autoroute in June, yet for the climaxes the temperatures are reversed. La Rochelle boils up to a frenzy in front of thousands whereas the road race fizzled out to only two survivors in its inaugural year.

The most recent addition, yet perhaps the trail blazer for all, is the Spartathlon. An imaginative concept to commemorate the longer version of Pheidippides' run, the inaugural race was held at the end of September 1983. Starting in Athens, an international field had first to negotiate the traffic of busy Greek highways before finding their way through wild mountain passes during the night. And, appropriately enough, it was a Greek who arrived in Sparta first. Yiannis Kouros took only 21 hr 53 min. 42 sec. to complete the 154 rugged miles—old Phei' has a worthy successor.

Training

If you are one of those athletes who has decided that Salazar and Joan Benoit are out of your reach, yet feel, when you cross the marathon finish line, that you could go further, you could well be of the stuff that ultra runners are made.

Training over 50 miles per week for several months can condition the body for more than just a marathon, and once you have run three or four in reasonable comfort, it is quite natural that you should look beyond that distance for your next challenge.

'Now what is reasonable comfort?' you may ask. It means having a bit to spare at the end and not being wiped out for a week. Ignore the 'out of puff' state you will be in after your sprint finish, and judge your condition by the way you feel and how many miles you can run the next day. If you manage a few and are relatively back to normal inside a week then you could well be capable of running beyond the marathon.

As our look into the past shows, it is not outrageous for human beings to cover vast distances on foot—indeed, when ultra runners finish a race they are often in better shape than their shorter-distance counterparts! So, far from being cranks, the long, slow merchants are in many ways smarter than the 'eye-balls out' brigade: they run at a more comfortable pace, suffer less strain and the satisfaction from finishing is greater.

But a look at the tactics of the past suggests that the

Opposite Australian farmer Cliff Young, 1983 winner of the Sydney–Melbourne race.

modern megamarathoner is not running slowly enough! Fed on a constant diet of 26.2 miles, with a few 40s and 50s for relish, today's runner does not know how to pace himself. Frequently he goes out and breaks records for the first couple of days but then he hits the wall. In a word, pacing is what running beyond the marathon is all about.

The old timers used to 'shuffle' along and mix running with walking, thus conserving their energy. Cliff Young 'shuffled' from Sydney to Melbourne and, if he had continued for six days, probably would have come the closest yet to Littlewood's 623¾ miles. Ann Sayer still holds the record from Land's End to John O'Groats (13 days, 17 hr 42 min.) and she walked every step of the way. Clearly, walking has a vital role to play in the very long races, but it is also extremely useful for the ultra novice who is building up his mileage.

As with other distances, there is no magic formula for the ultramarathon. There is, in fact, even more hard work and common sense required simply because you are out there longer and other aspects of life besides running are involved. And, like other distances, there is no absolute stereotype who runs this event. Apart from having slow-twitch muscles, ultra runners do not have a lot in common—they come in all shapes and sizes, backgrounds, temperaments, ages and ethnic groups. So it is no good thinking that because you are a slim, placid sort of Anglo-Saxon you are necessarily going to succeed. On the contrary, several fiery characters have excelled at the sport and provide interesting company during the long hours. Indeed, company is a big factor and for the novice it is a good idea to find some to start with.

Training on your own is fine for some people but can be a chore to others, whereas talking the miles away can be an excellent method of handling your first over-distance session. There you are on a Sunday morning tottering out on to that road, bleary eyed and stiff from a Saturday race or night on the town. You may think if you look half as bad as your mates, that there is no way you will even do a mile let alone 30 or whatever it is you have planned.

But then, as the chatter eases the cobwebs away, you are into your stride—not too fast for you have a long way to go and you want to keep talking, about the race or the night, about the week's work, about life in general. Now you are not feeling too bad and someone dares to mention another race. And suddenly there is new length in your stride as you look forward to the date.

You have forgotten the stiffness now and as you run down the quiet streets, milk still on doorsteps, papers still unread, population half asleep, you begin to appreciate how alive you feel yet you have no idea how far you have run. You do not care as you natter away, nineteen to the proverbial dozen, and suddenly

COMPLETE GUIDE TO RUNNING
COMPLETE GUIDE TO RUNNING

you have reached the turn around point—halfway, and yet you are only beginning to warm up.

Even if you struggle towards the end, even if you have to walk(!), do not worry; you are on your way and it is conversation that has cracked it. And as you relax in your bath looking forward to lunch, you can begin to call yourself an ultra runner.

Yes, that British sporting institution, the long Sunday run, can be the cornerstone of your training. Go with a good group who follow an interesting course and have watering holes laid on. These can be taps at service stations, in public parks or someone's house but, whatever the conditions, you *must* drink. Another purpose of the Sunday run is to hear the gossip and pick up tips on diet and injuries which sound more convincing from a fellow straggler on the

street. The whole experience can be enough to sustain your solo sojourns throughout the week.

Conversation is also one of the best guides to your pace and you should be able to pass the 'talk test' as you run; if you cannot, you must slow down rather than shut up. Talking really does not require that much effort and if you cannot manage it, you are obviously running too fast (in a race, of course, it is different as you will want to concentrate on your time).

Below The Frenchman Jean-Gilles Boussiquet, holder of the second furthest six-day distance of all time at La Rochelle in 1984. *Opposite* Joe Record, extrovert Australian with a huge appetite for beer and food, at La Rochelle.

So with a little help from your friends you could even cruise through your first over-distance training run wondering what all the fuss is about. But for those who find that fuss—and it is nothing to be ashamed of if you do—remember to walk. In fact for all but the supremely confident and experienced marathoner, walking should be an integral part of your early ultra preparations.

The trick is to walk *before* you are stiff. It may be difficult to stop in the middle of a steady run, but it is no good leaving the walk till the fatigue is with you —walking can only postpone fatigue not remove it. You need only walk for a few minutes, say five, and then start running again for another 20 minutes before reverting to a walk, and so on. The walk—at a reasonably brisk pace—will not only give you a respite from the pounding of the run but will have a therapeutic effect on the muscles.

Eventually, you may be able to eliminate the walking sessions altogether as they are merely to ease your way into the ultra scene, although, when it comes to the megamarathons, you may resort to them again. So walking and talking play big parts in your early ultra career and so, too, should thinking.

Many runners say that their other hobby is thinking—no wonder because there is certainly the time for it, but considerable thought has to go into your actual training session if it is one of those that takes the better part of the day. Doing a 50 or 60 miler can be fun as well as a fascinating experience but must be planned thoroughly. Ideally, you have a back-up vehicle but, assuming your 'second' is less enthusiastic about the enterprise than yourself, the best thing to do is to use your home as HQ. Work out various loops for variety and frequency of refreshment and start from your doorstep. You should also have changes of clothes available—they can make you feel better—even shoes if they are beginning to hurt, and getting out of the door again is all part of the test. Food, too, should be available, although eat only lightly, and a dip under the shower may freshen you up.

In these very long runs take particular notice of your fluid intake and use plenty of vaseline or cream on your more sensitive parts. Remember to wear light or reflective clothing in the dark and dress according to the temperature. You will begin to learn many of the tricks of the trade ready for your race.

Apart from the single spectacular long run that proves to you that you can do it, other ways of increasing your weekly mileage are simply to add the odd mile here and the odd loop there, either going around the park again or perhaps a longer way home. Fifteen more minutes a day can give you fifteen more miles in a week and could be the difference between handling one of the shorter ultras and hitting that familiar old wall. But once you have decided to 'up' your miles, those fives become sevens, those eights

ULTRA RECORDS	Six-Day professional	
623 miles 1320 yd	George Littlewood (GB)	New York 1888
621 miles 1320 yd	James A. Cathcart (USA)	New York 1888
610 miles 000 yd	Patrick Fitzgerald (USA)	New York 1884
605 miles 000 yd	Daniel Herty (USA)	New York 1888
602 miles 000 yd	Charles Rowell (GB)	New York 1884
600 miles 220 yd	George Hazael (GB)	New York 1882
590 miles 000 yd	Gus Guerrero (USA)	New York 1888
578 miles 440 yd	Robert Vint (USA)	New York 1881
568 miles 000 yd	John Hughes (USA)	New York 1881
567 miles 440 yd	George Noremac (GB)	New York 1882
	Six-Day amateur	
635 miles 1023 yd	Yiannis Kouros (Greece)	New York 1984
591 miles 1188 yd	Jean-Gilles Boussiquet (France)	La Rochelle 1984
581 miles 620 yd	Ramon Zabalo (France)	New York 1984
576 miles 675 yd	Tom O'Reilly (GB)	Nottingham 1982
571 miles 1164 yd	Stu Mittleman (USA)	La Rochelle 1984
554 miles 72 yd	George Gardiner (USA)	New York 1984
546 miles 1211 yd	Siegfried Bauer (New Zealand)	New York 1984
541 miles 1470 yd	Patrick Simonet (France)	La Rochelle 1984
539 miles 616 yd	Joe Record (Australia)	La Rochelle 1983
537 miles 561 yd	Ramon Zabalo (France)	La Rochelle 1982

Above *Eleanor Adams in the 1984 Danube Six-Day Race.* **Right** *Dave Dowdle, the 24-hour world record holder, running in the 1984 Nottingham Six-Day Race.*

run into tens, and 85 per week can be a 'ton' with no trouble at all.

Just because you are on a diet of high mileage it is no excuse to 'pig out'. You should eat more carbohydrates as your training increases but still be governed by your stomach. Generally ultra runners will eat more than any other sort—your metabolic rate will increase by training—but do not ask too much of it: you will only feel uncomfortable for your next run or be unable to sleep, which is something else you must get plenty of.

In order to sustain the increase in training, you will want to drop your pace by about half a minute per mile on the longer ones. That should see you through and still leave something for the shorter runs which should be tackled in the same old exuberant style. 'Moving up' is no reason to avoid racing, so you will still need that little bit of speed otherwise your stride will become shorter and the whole job a lot harder. Use short races (fives and tens) to put the spring back into your legs and use marathons as warm-ups for your ultra. Run a marathon about 15 minutes slower than your best and then you should be able to train normally the following week.

The final week before you race you should do very little—this is the period to taper. The hard work has

been done and all you can do now is ruin it by continuing to train by overeating and/or not sleeping. Enjoy a quiet, relaxing few days and avoid the pasta party. You can have all the celebrations you want *after* the race.

It remains only for the author to say that he hopes everyone finds ultramarathoning as rewarding an experience as he has.

Good luck and enjoy the journey.

Don Ritchie. Britain's greatest ultra runner of the past decade, the 39 year-old Scot is one of the country's most unassuming as well as unsung heroes. Holder of world records from 40 miles to 200km, Don's style is to go from the gun, a tactic which has also won him two 'Brightons' (1977 and 1978). In 1983 he won his first Scottish vest at the Aberdeen Marathon and in London dipped under 2 hr 20 min. for the first time. This Forres Harrier is a lecturer at a college in Elgin.

Tom O'Reilly. Until July 1984 he was the only runner of modern times to come within 50 miles of George Littlewood's six-day record. His 576 miles and 675 yd at Nottingham in 1982 was perhaps at that time the greatest ultra run of the century and the culmination of a career that has included a 4 min. 20 sec. mile, a 2 hr 20 min. marathon and 80,000 miles of training since 1959. Four times Midlands Marathon Champion and winner of the 'Brighton' in 1976, 39 year-old Tom is a school teacher and a member of Solihull and Small-heath Harriers.

Colin Dixon. At 45 this jovial Yorkshireman is the oldest member of the Six-Day '500 club' and his 520 miles 1234 yd at La Rochelle is the world record for his age group. That epic came only seven weeks after 482 miles at Nottingham—all done on a total of 12 hours' sleep! Gradually mastering the art of running while in a virtual trance, Colin again topped 500 miles in France in 1983, yet this East Hull Harrier has still to break 3 hr for the marathon.

Dave Dowdle. World record holder at both 24 and 48 hours (170 miles, 974 yd and 238 miles, 1122 yd respectively) this diminutive 29 year-old from Gloucester AC dominated long-distance track racing in 1982–83.

*Opposite Leslie Watson has completed 100 marathons. **Below** Colin Dixon, 45 years old and six-day world record holder for his age group.*

Below Don Ritchie, twice winner of the London to Brighton race.

50km		
2 hr 48 min. 06 sec.	Jeff Norman (Altrincham AC)	Timperley 1980
2 hr 50 min. 30 sec.	Don Ritchie (Forres H)	Timperley 1979
2 hr 52 min. 48 sec.	Barney Klecker (USA)	Tucson, Az 1981
2 hr 54 min. 44 sec.*	Jeff Julian (New Zealand)	Auckland 1969
2 hr 54 min. 54 sec.	Joe Keating (Ealing & Southall)	Uxbridge 1977
* Time at $31\frac{1}{4}$ miles/50.291 km		

50 miles		
4 hr 51 min. 49 sec.	Don Ritchie (Forres H)	Hendon 1983
4 hr 58 min. 53 sec.	Cavin Woodward (Leamington CAC)	Tipton 1975
5 hr 01 min. 01 sec.	Phil Hampton (Royal Navy AC)	Ewell 1971
5 hr 05 min. 30 sec.	Tom O'Reilly (Small Heath)	London 1975
5 hr 12 min. 40 sec.	Alan Phillips (Norfolk Gazelles)	Walton 1966

100km		
6 hr 10 min. 20 sec.	Don Ritchie (Forres H)	London 1978
6 hr 25 min. 28 sec.	Cavin Woodward (Leamington CAC)	Tipton 1975
6 hr 40 min. 20 sec.	Vito Melito (Italy)	Bologna 1982
6 hr 43 min. 59 sec.	Tom O'Reilly (Small Heath)	London 1976
6 hr 44 min. 42 sec.	Mike Newton (South London H)	London 1976

100 miles		
11 hr 30 min. 51 sec.	Don Ritchie (Forres H)	London 1977
11 hr 38 min. 54 sec.	Cavin Woodward (Leamington CAC)	Tipton 1975
11 hr 56 min. 56 sec.	Derek Kay (South Africa)	Durban 1972
12 hr 02 min. 32 sec.	Tom O'Reilly (Small Heath)	Tipton 1975
12 hr 15 min. 09 sec.	Dave Box (South Africa)	Durban 1970

Kelvin Bowers. Holds the record for the longest ever run—10,289 miles from Stoke-on-Trent to Sydney! It took him 552 actual running days and he survived stonings, earthquakes, rebellions and disease through some of Earth's less hospitable regions. Supporting him throughout were his wife and three-year-old son, and with the speed to run a 4 min. 12 sec. mile and 2 hr 33 min. marathon, this 37 year-old Potteries Marathon Athletic Club member could claim to be the complete runner.

Joe Record. This extrovert Aussie (by way of Yorkshire and Ranelagh Harriers) is a true Bohemian of the running scene. His 539 miles 616 yd in 1983 was the first time he has come close to realizing his full potential as he possesses immense strength and distance running know-how. Prone to 'walkabouts' during races, this 42 year-old has a great capacity for beer and food. Other notable performances have been in the 'Sydney to Melbourne', and a journey run from Perth to Kalgoorlie (372 miles in five days).

Cliff Young. Took Australia by storm when he won the inaugural Sydney to Melbourne road race in 1983, covering the 537 miles in $5\frac{1}{2}$ days on a diet of pumpkins and potatoes, and with virtually no sleep.

He only started running four years ago and is reputed to have trained by chasing cows around his farm in Wellington boots. This 62-year-old from Colac, Victoria, is now a national hero.

Yiannis Kouros. Having won the first ever Spartathlon race in 1983, he broke George Littlewood's 96 year old record for a six-day event at New York in July 1984 with 635 miles 1023 yd. He ran a staggering 266 miles 1016 yd in the first two days!

Jean-Gilles Boussiquet. A former footballer who broke Ron Bentley's long standing 24 hour record in 1981 and also held the 48 hour mark; yet to realize full potential over six days, but still a folk hero in his native France.

Ramon Zabalo. Tough Toulouse riot policeman who won the first six-day race ever held in France with 537 miles 561 yd. He also held the 48 hour mark but seldom races outside France.

Leslie Watson. World record holder at 50 miles (6 hr 20 min. 42 sec.) and Britain's most prolific lady marathoner. With her looks and personality, the Scottish physiotherapist is a popular figure on the road running circuit and will, in 1984, complete her one hundredth marathon.

Eleanor Adams. A Nottinghamshire housewife and mother of three who now holds more world records than any other British athlete. Indoors she holds everything from 30 miles to 24 hours, while outdoors the Sutton Harrier holds the 50km and has held the 'six-day', which at 408 miles 1625 yd is perhaps her best distance.

Lynn Fitzgerald. Despite being a late developer and having only one lung, Lynn, who is a leading researcher on arthritis, has collected several world bests; she has held the 100km (8 hr 39 min. 10 sec.) and currently holds the 100 mile (15 hr 44 min. 21 sec.) record.

Bruce Fordyce. Generally regarded as the greatest ultra runner of all time, in 1983 this 28 year-old South African with a British passport completed an undreamed-of double hat-trick: he won the 'Com-

rades' and the 'Brighton' in the same year for the third time in a row! Has also run a 2 hr 17 min. marathon at altitude yet took to running late when he felt unfit playing rugby. An archaeology research officer with Wits University in Johannesburg, Bruce has been nominated for the South African Sports Personality of the Year.

Mike Newton. Became the first man of modern times to break the 500 mile barrier in a six-day race. 'Newtonian mileage' is now part of the ultra running vernacular as the 39-year-old South London Harrier regularly tots up 300-mile weeks running to such places as Brighton and Windsor from his Streatham home. Once, when asked where he trained, Mike replied: 'In southern England.' Not bad for a 180 lb fatty who, ten years ago, preferred to keep wicket rather than run around the cricket field. Since then this unmarried security officer has held the world 200km record as well as many multi-day marks, winning major ultras at home and abroad. Although he has run a 'ten' in 53 min. and a marathon in 2 hr 29 min., he felt at the 1000 mile charity run in 1983 that he had finally found his distance.

24 hours		
274.480 km 170 miles 974 yd	Dave Dowdle (Gloucester AC)	Gloucester 1982
272.624 km 169 miles 705 yd	Jean-Gilles Boussiquet (France)	Lausanne 1981
263.466 km 163 miles 1249 yd	Mark Pickard (Epsom & Ewell)	Hendon 1981
261.204 km 162 miles 537 yd	Park Barner (USA)	Huntington Bh 1979
259.603 km 161 miles 545 yd	Ron Bentley (Tipton H)	Walton 1973

48 hours		
384.050 km 238 miles 1122 yd	Dave Dowdle (Gloucester AC)	Gloucester 1983
381.600 km 237 miles 202 yd	Jean-Gilles Boussiquet (France)	Montauban 1983
368.370 km 228 miles 1574 yd	Jean-Pierre Haec (France)	Gloucester 1983
368.348 km 228 miles 1550 yd	Ramon Zabalo (France)	Toulouse 1982
365.623 km 227 miles 330 yd	Mike Newton (South London H)	Nottingham 1982

Road bests		
50 km 2 hr 48 min. 52 sec.	Ben Choeu (South Africa)	Pretoria 1981
50 miles 4 hr 50 min. 21 sec.	Bruce Fordyce (South Africa)	Brighton 1983
100 km 6 hr 28 min. 11 sec.	Don Ritchie (Forres H)	Santander 1982
100 miles 11 hr 51 min. 12 sec.	Don Ritchie	Queens, NY 1979
24 hr 170 miles 1231 yd	Bernard Gaudin (France)	Niort 1982
Six-day 536 miles	Cliff Young (Australia)	Sydney–Melbourne 1983

* Note although Ritchie, Woodward and Kamenik have faster road marks, the above is the fastest on a certified course.

Female ultra bests		
50 km 3 hr 44 min. 08 sec.	Eleanor Adams (Sutton-in-Ashfield)	Bingham 1982
50 miles 6 hr 20 min. 42 sec.	Leslie Watson (London Olympiades)	Hendon 1983
100 km 8 hr 1 min. 1 sec.	Monika Kuho (West Germany)	Vogt 1983
100 miles 15 hr 44 min. 21 sec.	Lynn Fitzgerald (Highgate H)	Nottingham 1983
24 hr 134 miles 1089 yd	Ros Paul (Barnet Ladies)	Nottingham 1982
48 hr 186 miles 623 yd	Ros Paul	Nottingham 1982
6 days 472 miles 1300 yd	E. Couché (France)	La Rochelle 1984

Clothing and equipment

Purpose

Including footwear, as clothing for feet, let us first of all consider what is the purpose of clothing. We can identify the following functions.

1 Identification and decoration. Teams have their own colours to separate them from other teams and individuals, and usually these colours are sufficiently decorative for their owners to be proud and happy to wear them. Individuals, where possible, will select smart, well designed, nicely coloured clothing to match their personalities. They want to look good to feel good. Certain 'harrier runners', luckily (for business) only a few, have other ideas!

2 Modesty. It would create quite a stir if people started running nude, although apart from having nowhere to pin the number, this may be the ideal way to run on a hot day! However, there are rules against it. Men as well as women must wear singlets. You might declare that you do not see a man's bare chest as being immodest, but many of our amateur athletic rules date back to the days of Victorian standards. All can see the point of the rule that says men's shorts must be of such a material that they are not transparent when wet!

3 Protection. This is most important in footwear where protection from hard, rough surfaces is essential, but in clothing we would look towards protection of the body against cold, wet, and sometimes heat.

In examining what is available to the runner, it is perhaps better to start at the bottom and work upwards, then outwards!

Footwear

Shoes are the most important piece of running equipment you will keep having to buy. They can add pleasure to your running if you can forget you are wearing them, and they function well. Or, they can make your training hell if you pick a pair that do not suit you and you persevere with them.

Fit. The best advice for the novice, when wanting to select a shoe, is to ask around among friends or colleagues and then, armed with a little advice, go along to a specialist running shop and ask for advice again. Then try some shoes on, walk around the store in them, make sure they are comfortable and be certain that there is enough room for your feet to swell slightly, which is what happens when you actually start to run. Once you have some experience, possibly gained by the odd mistake, you will be more

Ron Hill Sports' latest design in running shoes: note the cutaway heel protector designed to avoid pressure on the Achilles tendon.

capable of making the right choice. 'If the shoe fits, wear it' is a good adage!

Selection by price. Avoid cheap unknown brands. These are 'trainers', poseurs' shoes, not meant to give you lasting protection. And avoid the most expensive shoes, unless you are absolutely convinced. A lot of the price may be due to dollar versus pound fluctuations, rather than technical input into the shoes! You get what you pay for, up to a point, and you will soon ascertain what the average shoe costs by comparison of the models available. If it costs a lot above average, you will want to know why.

Selection by quality. When selecting any shoe for training or racing, ensure that there is sufficient cushioning for your weight, that there is a good stiff plastic heel counter inside the shoe, which will hold your foot firm at the back and not collapse over with time, that there is plenty of room in the toe-box , so that your toes do not get squashed, then minced as you run, and that the shoe bends easily in the middle.

Selection for purpose. Many people try to make do with one pair of shoes, both training in them and racing in them, but it makes for far more pleasurable running if you have more than one pair, even if only to be able to put on a dry pair the day after a run through mud, slush or rain.

A suggestion is to keep, as a minimum, six pairs of shoes on the go, in the following categories:

1. Training shoes, morning: multipurpose road/trail shoe or road shoe.
2. Training shoes, afternoon: multipurpose road/trail shoe or road shoe.
3. Sunday (or other) long run: racer/trainer shoe (lightweight).
4. Road racing/marathon: lightweight road racing shoe.
5. Track/cross country: lightweight spiked shoe.
6. Fell racing: lightweight studded shoe.

As the last four types of shoe are only worn for occasional and special purposes they could well last for 18 months (categories 3 and 4), and two or three years (categories 5 and 6).

Training shoes are the ones which wear out quickest, especially if you are a high mileage person, but there is little that can be done about it, unless technology comes up with a super-hardwearing, resilient new substance.

Returning to the ideal list of shoes, the following describe the main features of the various categories.

Road shoe. These will have a shallow profile on the sole and you would expect to slip about if you ran on a muddy path. Typically the weight for one size 8 shoe would be 250–340 grammes (9–12 oz).

Multipurpose road/trail shoe. These have a fairly deep profile system of studs, bars or other protuberances on the outersole in order to give grip and traction on muddy surfaces, obviously useful for snow or slush conditions. One size 8 shoe would weigh 250–340 grammes (9–12 oz).

Racer/trainer shoes. These usually have the shallow profiled outersole of a road shoe and weigh about 250 grammes (9 oz) for one size 8 shoe. They are for long road runs, or mixed runs under relatively dry conditions, and are preferred by heavy runners for racing.

Road race shoes. The feature of these shoes is their lightness in weight, and some tip the scales at a mere 160 grammes for one size 8 shoe.

Spikes. Essential for track runners and serious cross-country runners. There are still many cinder tracks for which long 'regular' (as opposed to 'needle') spikes are needed. Spikes are available in lengths from 5mm to 18mm and the harder the track, the shorter the spikes needed. All shoes these days have a spike plate at the front of the shoe into which the individual spikes themselves can be screwed and unscrewed. There are usually seven holes, but only six spikes are allowed by the rules and a blank fills the spare hole. Sprint spiked shoes could accommodate a rounded heel profile as sprinters are on their toes all the time, whereas middle- and long-distance runners prefer a thin wedge-shaped heel at the back. Hence the availability of 'sprint' and 'distance' options in the top of the range of models. Less expensive spikes tend to be multipurpose.

The reason for spikes is obvious: they give grip by digging into the track or ground surface but, additionally, spiked shoes are always light (160–210 grammes (6–7½ oz)) as they are usually reserved for racing.

For racing on synthetic tracks, small needle-like spikes are all that are necessary; in fact some 'spikes' for these tracks are not pointed at all, but flat ended to avoid puncturing the surface of the track.

Racing cross-country, especially in muddy conditions, necessitates spikes and 12mm or 15mm lengths are mostly used. The wetter the ground, the longer the spikes needed. Usually, regular track spikes will be adequate, although there are special spiked shoes on the market with studded rear soles for extra grip.

Studs. Most commonly required by orienteers and fell runners but sometimes used in cross-country. They usually have deep, well spaced studs to give maximum grip in muddy or loose terrain, especially when running downhill. Some companies attempt to provide a waterproof upper and, by and large, the shoes are heavy for competition purposes. The market awaits a really excellent racing stud.

Heavy versus light shoes. This is usually a matter of personal preference. A medium-weight shoe can be used for a long run, but, for normal training, a heavier shoe can strengthen the legs and gives a favourable contrast when changing into light racing shoes.

Ladies' shoes. Some companies have introduced shoes built on special women's lasts which they report are narrower than men's. As far as the UK market is concerned the majority of women runners appear to find the small sized shoes built on standard lasts quite suitable. If they require cosmetic changes, that is, fashionable feminine colours, this need is also being catered for by most companies.

Special problems

On reading athletics magazines and shoe manufacturers' literature, or in conversation with other runners, the terms 'pronation', 'supination', and 'orthotics' may well be encountered, and the meaning of these words will be explained briefly below.

Pronation. Both pronation and supination are normal in a runner's gait, or action, and they are part of the body's natural biomechanical cushioning process. Most runners land on the outside of their heels, from which position the foot rolls over, so that the weight is transferred to the inside of the foot. When this motion becomes excessive we have 'over-pronation', and this is where the problems arise as over-rolling has to be compensated by movements further up the legs and skeleton. Many injuries can arise through over-pronation, most notably knee pains.

Supination. This involves movement at the front of the foot, from the inside to the outside, and excessive motion is 'over-supination', though this is nowhere near as common as over-pronation.

Orthotics. Where foot or leg imbalance occurs, or other gait problems, it is now possible to construct custom-made shoe inserts, which are built up in specific areas, in order to correct imbalances during the running action. Many athletes have found that orthotics have cured long-standing injury problems.

Contemporary footwear. It is possible that today's shoes are responsible for many injury problems, including over-pronation, and at least one shoe company is examining a solution to this dilemma.

Main picture *Running shoe manufacture combines traditional shoe-making techniques and high technology.* *Inset* *The typical construction of a modern shoe.* *Opposite top* *This is a highly developed pair of spikes designed with plastic inserts and wedges for running on synthetic tracks.* *Opposite middle* *Lightweight racing/tracing shoe.* *Opposite bottom* *Training shoe with a durable non-slip sole and breathable mesh uppers.*

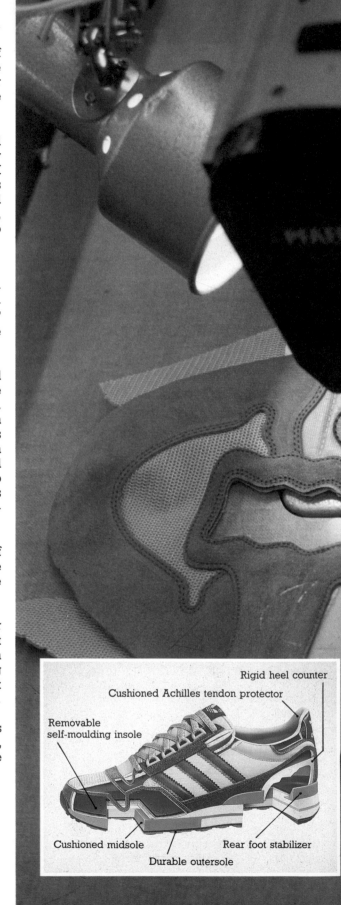

Rigid heel counter

Cushioned Achilles tendon protector

Removable self-moulding insole

Cushioned midsole

Durable outersole

Rear foot stabilizer

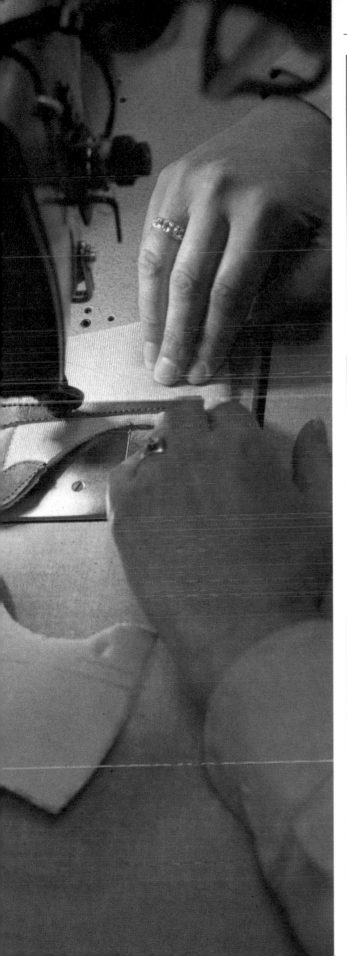

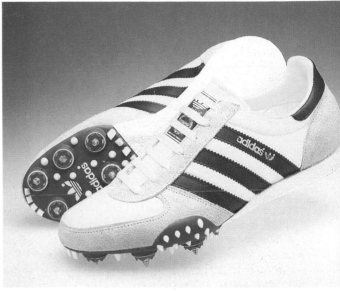

Shoe care

In about 1972, there was a rapid swing away from leather upper shoes to nylon uppers, and what a boon that was for runners—no more bending and cracking and, as a last resort, rewetting of dried-out leather shoes.

Nylon shoes could be worn in the wet, or washed, and they dried up pretty well as soft as when new. When shoes get very dirty or sweaty they can be washed in a dilute detergent, scrubbing them with a soft scrubbing brush, then rinsing them thoroughly. They *can* be put in the washing machine on a warm wash, and they come out very well. The replaceable insoles, so popular now, can be washed and dried independently if necessary.

Spikes tend to be a much snugger, tighter fit than training shoes, and after washing the mud of a cross-country race from them, it is a good idea to stuff them with newspaper to prevent them shrinking. It is not the nylon that shrinks on drying but the suede leather 'facings' around the front of the shoe.

Future shoes

So much has gone on in the last decade in relation to shoe design, that it is difficult to imagine what further developments are left. Rest assured, that with the competition between shoe companies being so fierce, the setting up of research departments within shoe companies, and the continuing explosion of technology, there is a long way to go yet.

Socks

The functions of socks are five fold: (1) they provide a desirable aesthetic appearance (2) they fill up the spaces between the foot and the shoe, holding the foot firmly and protecting the skin from pressure points of the shoe that may lead to blisters (3) they are claimed in some cases to provide extra cushioning (4) they provide warmth to the foot, the ankle and the Achilles tendon (5) they plug the gap between the ankle and the inside of the shoe, keeping out uncomfortable mud when running over wet fields or trails.

At one time socks were nigh on essential, but with shoes built the way they are now, they feel almost like slippers and in summer socks may well be unnecessary for the majority of runners.

There used only to be 'sports socks' on the market, but now there is a bewildering array as hosiery manufacturers have hurried to take their share of the running boom. Here we shall list the main categories of sock available, and it is then up to the runner to choose which type suits his purpose best.

Above right Lightweight winter training gear. *Below right* Winter training gear. Lightweight tracksters and long sleeve shirts specially designed for training in cold conditions. *Opposite left* Jogging suits ideal for warming up and for after the race. *Opposite right* Shorts and singlets come in a variety of styles and should be chosen for comfort rather than fashion.

Yarn materials. The most common materials you will find in socks are cotton, nylon (polyamide), acrylic, or wool. Cotton is very comfortable, but absorbs water and therefore gets heavy when wet. This means cotton socks are difficult to dry after washing. Cotton also wears out very quickly, especially when wet, but it is often blended or mixed with a small amount of nylon to add strength. Nylon has good stretch and recovery properties and is easy to care for, the only disadvantage being that it may feel a little harsh. Acrylics are generally soft but, like cotton, are physically weak and wear out quickly unless reinforced with nylon. Acrylics are generally at the cheaper end of the market. Wool is not found as a 100% fibre in running socks but may be used as a blend, for instance with nylon in the cushion sole of socks.

Construction. There are four main considerations in the construction of socks: (1) cushion sole (with loops of yarn to provide a thicker bed, and usually extending around the toes and heel for extra comfort and durability) or plain sole; (2) light-weight or regular weight; (3) high-cut or low-cut; depending on weather, the leg of the sock extends well over the ankle, to the ankle, or just under the ankle bones; (4) seamed toe or linked toe, the latter being preferable in any choice as this provides a flat join at the toe of the sock, minimizing the chances of abrasion and hence blisters.

The choices are fairly obvious depending on what you need the socks for and, perhaps, what you can afford. For racing you will need low-cut, lightweight socks, and at the other extreme, for training in cold muddy weather, a high-cut cushioned soled sock in cotton or nylon, with or without wool in the sole.

Shorts

Gone are the days of long, baggy, stiff shorts made from woven materials. Now we have soft knitted-material shorts, action cut with built-in briefs for men and similar styled shorts for women, or alternatively brief shorts in soft stretch materials.

Some men prefer to wear the traditional jock-strap, some have moved on to nylon or other types of brief, and for these runners there are still many 'shell' type (that is without built-in-brief) shorts on the market.

The largest share of the running market is taken by shorts made from tricot-knitted nylon which is light, non-restrictive and easy to care for. There is still a feeling for cotton among the public and shorts in woven polyester/cotton blends (the polyester adds great strength to the cloth) are still popular and available.

The styling of shorts has developed considerably over the last 15 years, with the advent of the wrap-over style of short, which allows the front and back panels to slide over each other when the leg stretches forward. Before that, shorts were restrictive and tended to grab at the front of the thigh as the material

had to slide over the skin to allow movement.

An alternative to this, now that values of modesty have changed, is to have a very brief short so that there is no material hanging down the leg.

Many women runners are switching to 'short-type' shorts, in tricot knitted nylon, as an alternative to the traditional racing shorts, as these look far more 'normal' for training runs, and can double up for leisure or beach wear.

When choosing a pair of shorts, try them on in the shop. Do you look good in them? Lift up your knees. Do they feel restrictive in any way? Once you have made a purchase wash them and run in them for two or three weeks before you race in them.

Singlets

Singlets are available in a whole range of materials and combinations. Cotton, polyester/cotton, polyester/Viloft (a special rayon), stretch nylon, tricot knitted nylon, mesh in several materials, and part-mesh/part-nylon combinations.

100% cotton should be avoided where possible as

*Above The Nike international laboratories researching into running shoes. **Opposite** Shoe tests carried out on the Nike rolling road.*

these singlets get extremely heavy when wet, are hard to dry, and lose their shape eventually. For cold weather choose a poly/cotton poly/Viloft, or nylon interlock singlet or wear one of the lighter-weight types over a T-shirt or long sleeve shirt.

For warm weather, choose a lightweight singlet, with mesh or in all mesh (for men!) if you expect to compete on a very hot day.

Again, after making a choice, try the singlet on, breathe in deeply, and move your arms around. If there are no restrictions you can safely buy it.

T-shirts

For less serious runners, these are all-the-year-round racing wear and usually carry some kind of slogan, advertising or proof of having been somewhere exotic! Fine. For the serious runner, they are a useful

garment for training in both cool or cold weather; in cool weather, possibly the T-shirt alone; in cold weather, as a garment under something else, such as a tracksuit or foul weather suit.

Long sleeve shirts

These are useful for competition if they are close fitting and non-restrictive (see next section on Thermal wear) and it is usual to wear a singlet over the top. They are also useful under a tracksuit, or weather suit, as an extra layer for warmth.

Thermal wear

The use of thermal wear in running has been turned inside out. The garments which are being marketed, that is T-shirts, long sleeve shirts and leg tights, can be worn under garments, but most commonly they are used by runners as protection for exposed limbs in extremely cold weather, and the tights are worn under shorts, and long sleeve shirts under competition singlets.

The materials most commonly encountered are polypropylene, polyester, or a blend of polyester and Viloft.

Sweatshirts

Sweatshirts come in several fibres and blends, including 100% cotton, cotton/polyester, cotton/acrylic, 100% acrylic, and polyester/rayon. Like a T-shirt, it is a leisure/active garment, often sporting large logos. They have 'fleece' linings, produced by 'raising' (mechanically scratching up the back of the fabric) and hence tend to be warm. With a hood and a pouch pocket the sweatshirt becomes a jog-top.

Tracksuits

Tracksuits, once upon a time, were training suits and as such were tailored for running. They had tapered legs on the trousers and elasticated welts on the jackets, so that they did not flap about. Nowadays there are few training suits on the market, and the tracksuits that are available are more pre- or après-activity suits in smart and fashion-conscious styles and colours, very often with 'parallel' legs, which flap about when running. However, they do keep you warm before and after a race or training session, and as such are an essential part of the runner's wardrobe. Clubs and countries often have tracksuits in special colours as part of a uniform.

The suits can come in an amazing variety of fibres and blends, and one should look for something with nylon in it, usually, which will give the suit stretch and recovery properties. However, there are satisfactory 'uniform' suits made from 100% polyester, and polyester with cotton. At the top end of the 'poseur' market you will find blends of nylon/acetate, polyester/acetate, nylon/cotton and even wool/acrylic blends.

Jogsuits

Jogsuits can be an inexpensive substitute for a tracksuit, the ease of movement in these garments coming from the baggy nature of the cut. Cuffs at the bottoms of the legs prevent them from catching the feet when running.

Training-bottoms

These garments have filled a gap in the market which appeared when tracksuits with tapered legs virtually disappeared. Even if these types of suit were still easily accessible, separate training bottoms would be just as necessary as, with these suits, the bottoms always wear out first.

Training bottoms are available in different fabrics but probably the best and certainly the best known are 'Tracksters' (TM), made from lightweight stretch nylon, which keep the legs warm, yet offer little resistance or restriction when running. Being 100% nylon, they are easily washed and dried. Matching Trackster tops are also made which, together with the bottoms, give an excellent lightweight training suit.

Weather-suits

Weather-suits of great variety are on the market and, certainly for winter wear, they are being worn more and more instead of tracksuits. They vary considerably in their performance, from those that keep out the wind, to those that are waterproof and keep out the elements completely. There is also a considerable variety in price.

The ones that keep out the wind only are obviously not going to offer a great deal of protection from rain, and this has to be remembered when making a purchase. Rainsuits themselves vary a lot in performance. Some lightly coated or proofed nylon suits will keep the wearer dry for a short amount of time in rain, but eventually water will soak through. Heavily proofed fabrics will keep water out, but also keep water, i.e. perspiration, in. But this is usually all right because at least you will be WARM and wet inside, with the cold rain on the outside. You have to rely on layers of clothing inside these rainsuits to soak up perspiration. However, even with waterproof fabrics, rain will penetrate the seams, where the holes of the sewing threads occur, unless these seams are specially treated.

Other fabrics are on the market which claim to 'breathe', that is, they have a layer of material in the construction which contains microscopic holes. These holes are too small to allow liquid water to penetrate, but large enough to allow molecules of water vapour to pass through. Theoretically this means rain stays on the outside, yet perspiration vapour is transmitted from the inside to the out. This may well be the case for activities like strolling, but, when running produces liquid perspiration, this stays put on the inside. But still you stay warm, and, in the author's experience, comfortable. The best product in this range of fabrics is Goretex (TM).

There are other in-between suits made from proofed polyester/cotton/nylon blend fabrics, with a mesh lining to the body, which 'breathe', and which have enjoyed considerable success.

When looking at the price of weather-suits, the more that goes into it, or the better the performance, the more you have to pay. The very best suits are quite expensive.

Accessories

The accessories available to runners vary from the useful to the essential, and the main products are covered below.

Reflective gear

These are in the 'essential' category for running on dark nights. The 'Run-a-Brite' range comprises a slip-over singlet with reflective strips and a reflective armband. Also available are armbands with flashing lights!

Gloves

If your hands are warm, you feel warm all over. Lightweight Viloft gloves are ideal for training and racing but if the temperature is well below freezing woolly gloves may well be necessary.

Hats

Woolly hats can be useful in very cold weather and at the other extreme many people like to wear a peaked cap in hot sunny weather.

Pouches

Small pouches, which can be strapped around the waist, are popular with those people who commute to and from work on foot, or need to carry things on a long run e.g. maps, money, drinks, camera, etc. Larger, rucksack type bags are also available for people who may want to carry something more bulky e.g. clothing.

Jog-bras

These are specially designed for sportswomen to give firm support and anchorage, and are ideally suited for women runners.

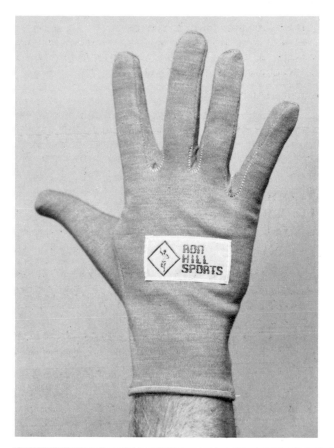

Above right Lightweight running glove, suitable for all but the coldest weather. ***Below right*** These weather suits (manufactured by Ron Hill Sports) are ideal for training in wet and windy conditions.

Index

References to illustrations are in italics

Picture acknowledgements

Adidas 166 inset, 167; Associated Press 8 bottom, 9 top, 59, 144, 152;
BBC Hulton Picture Library 8 top, 9 bottom left and right, 53, 68, 104,
105; David Billington 148; David Hoffman 94–95, 121; Peter Loughran
6–7, 30–31, 34, 44, 58, 88, 98, 126–127, 162–163; Noël Manchée 99, 101
top; The Mansell Collection 80 left, 81, 96–97, 97, 117; Mary Evans
Picture Library 80 right; Nike International 13 left, 15, 17, 166–167, 170,
171; Howard Payne 19, 20, 21, 22, 23, 24 top and bottom, 25, 26, 27, 28,
29, 30 inset, 33, 72, 73, 74, 75, 76, 77; Stuart Perry 100 bottom; Ron Hill
Sports 164, 168, 169, 173; Mark Shearman, 2–3, 4–5, 10–11, 12, 13 right,
14 right, 16, 39, 40, 42, 43, 45, 47, 49, 50–51, 52, 55, 56–57, 60–61, 62, 63,
64, 65, 66–67, 69, 70, 71, 78–79, 82–83, 84–85, 85, 86, 87 top and bottom,
89, 90–91, 91, 92–93, 102–103, 106, 106–107, 108–109, 109, 110–111, 111
inset, 112, 113, 114–115, 118, 119, 122–123, 124, 125, 127 inset bottom,
128–129, 130, 131, 132, 133, 134, 135, 136, 137, 138–139, 146, 147, 149,
151, 158, 159 bottom right; Bruce and Ceridwen Slade 143, 145, 154,
155, 157, 159; Ian Weightman 140, 141, 142.
Front cover photograph by Peter Loughran.